REMEDY

THE ANSWER TO EVERY PROBLEM KNOWN TO MAN

Father Lawrence Carney

CARITAS PRESS, ARIZONA, USA

REMEDY
The Answer to Every Problem Known to Man

Nihil Obstat: Rev. Thomas Hoisington, S.T.L.
                Censor Librorum
Imprimatur: +The Most Reverend. Carl A. Kemme, D.D.
                Bishop of Wichita, Kansas
                November 3, 2021

Father Lawrence Carney
Copyright © 2020 by Father Lawrence Carney

Back cover photo: Frieda Larson
Front Cover photo: Jon-Paul Lohrentz
Fr. Andrew Bergkamp celebrating Holy Mass at St. Joseph Parish, Wichita, Kansas
Cover and Interior Design: Sherry Boas

Names have been changed throughout to protect identities.

No part of this publication may be reproduced, stored in a retrieval system or transmitted in any form or by any means, electronic, mechanical, photocopying, recording or otherwise without written permission of the publisher.
For information regarding permission, contact Sherry@LilyTrilogy.com

First Edition 10 9 8 7 6 5 4 3 2 1
ISBN: 978-1-940209-40-1

CARITAS PRESS
CaritasPress.org

Dedication

TO THE HOLY FACE OF JESUS

Face of our Redeemer who saves us,

Who, "...looked on Peter. And Peter remembered the word of the Lord, as He had said: Before the cock crow they shalt deny me thrice. And Peter going out, wept bitterly."

— Luke xxii. 61-62

THIS WORK IS LOVINGLY AND HUMBLY DEDICATED
BY THE AUTHOR

PRAYER OF BL. POPE PIUS IX

O my Jesus! cast upon us a look of mercy; turn Thy face toward each one of us, even as Thou didst turn toward Veronica, not that we may see it with eyes of our body, for we do not deserve to do so, but turn it towards our hearts, that being sustained by Thee, we may ever draw from that powerful source, the vigour necessary to enable us to wage the combats we have to undergo.

10 MARCH 1872

AUTHOR'S NOTE

    I was asked to write a book about how all the problems of the world can be answered by the Catholic Church. After thinking about how to tackle such a work of magnificent proportions, I asked a certain Cardinal of the Catholic Church. His Eminence told me, "Go to the Summa of St. Thomas and you will find the answers in the table of contents." With that answer I was ready to embark on the journey of writing this book.

    Pope Leo XIII in his encyclical Aeterni Patris (1879) summarizes his praise of the great Angelic Doctor St. Thomas Aquinas. "Among the scholastic doctors, the chief and master of all, towers Thomas Aquinas, who, as Cajetan observes, because 'he has venerated the ancient doctors of the Church, in a certain way seems to have inherited the intellect of all'." He goes on to list his predecessors in the Roman pontificate who have celebrated the wisdom of St. Thomas Aquinas: Clement VI, Nicholas V, Benedict XIII, St. Pius V, Clement XII, Blessed Urban V, Innocent XII, Benedict XIV, and finally Innocent VI who said, "His teaching above that of others, the canons alone excepted, enjoys such an elegance of phraseology, a method of statement, a truth of proposition, that those who hold to it were never found swerving from the path of truth, and he who dare assail it will always be suspected of error" (Serm. de St. Thom.). Many Popes also required St. Thomas to be taught by all seminaries. As the world continues to plunge into the darkness of error, St. Thomas is ever more needed by not only scholars, seminarians and clerics, but he also needs to be known by all. That is why I decided to sprinkle in stories that I encountered while walking the streets of the world. My hope is that the common man Catholic or not will be popularly exposed to the great mind of St. Thomas. Often I listen to people in the streets regarding their problems and their errors. In this book, I cite the encounter and leave the unfinished story as a "cliffhanger." Then I apply St. Thomas and/or other Saints and sound theologians to give the answer to the problem. Then I end by finishing the story. Some endings are good and some are bad.

Just like our lives that will either end in heaven or hell; this is the Christian drama par excellence in each person.

The reason I dedicate this book to the Holy Face is varied. First imagine the Face of Jesus, "...turning looked on Peter. And Peter remembered the word of the Lord, as he had said: Before the cock crow, thou shalt deny me thrice. And Peter going out, wept bitterly" (Lk. xxii. 61-62). Imagine being like Peter, denying Our Lord. We all have done it. Imagine receiving the grace of Peter seeing the Face of love and truth. His Face was mentioned in Scripture as shining like the sun, bathed in a bloody sweat, betrayed by the kiss of Judas, received a blow from the hand of a servant, was veiled, covered with spittle, wounded with blows and crowned with thorns. Every time we fall and come back to God it is like the grace of St. Peter, our first Pope. In fact of the twelve Apostles, one took his life, ten fled from the cross and only one, St. John was with Jesus the whole time at the foot of the Cross. We have to remember the Church was full of weak men including the first Pope. We are all weak too and are in need of Jesus to show us His Face so that we can be saved. The Blessed Virgin Mary in her solitude interceded for these weak men to receive the grace to come back to the Way. We in our times need to beg Jesus to show us His Face. We need missionaries to show their faces once again to all, and by these encounters, be directed to the Holy Face of Jesus.

St. Francis Xavier said, "It often comes to my mind to go around all the Universities of Europe, and especially that of Paris, crying out everywhere like a madman, and saying to all the learned men there whose learning is so much greater than their charity, 'Ah! what a multitude of souls is through your fault shut out of heaven and falling into hell!' Would to God that these men who labor so much in gaining knowledge would give as much thought to the account they must one day give to God of the use they have made of their learning and of the talents entrusted to them!" (The Life and Letters of St. Francis Xavier, Henry James Coleridge.) Since writing my first book with stories of the people I encounter, I am edified at the number of priests, religious and lay people who are literally going out armed with their Rosaries in an attempt to show the face of the Church to save souls from plunging into hell. Oh that we could be like St. Francis Xavier whose love for God was so great that it is said that he baptized millions of souls in the Indies. Although our numbers are meager, we are at least trying.

I have been going around the world encouraging people to pray for the gifts of the Holy Spirit, the fruits of the Holy Spirit, the virtues and the prayer of contemplation. St. Francis loved God so much that he was privileged with so many miracles, principalities and kings would flock to him asking if he would baptize their tribes. We too can be disposed for this grace if we approach the mission field again with charity and truth, like St. Francis Xavier and St. Thomas. One way is for groups of people to form and gather regularly to pray from the Manual of the Archconfraternity of the Holy Face.

Pope Leo XIII confirmed the revelations given by Jesus to Sr. Mary St. Peter in the 1840s and elevated the Confraternity of the Holy Face to the status of an Archconfraternity in 1885. One of the first members was St. Theresa of Lisieux who continues to be an apostle in heaven raining down roses from heaven. Armed with groups dedicated to prayer as members of the Most Holy Rosary and the Archconfraternity of the Holy Face, I hope that God provides us with a movement that brings about the triumph of the Church as Our Lady of Fatima promised through her Immaculate Heart that goes out into the streets like Jesus did to save souls. The Catholic Church was instituted by Jesus Christ to save souls. May She fulfill this charge with proportions unlike any century before. May this book inspire that movement in the hearts and intellects of men!

CONTENTS

1	Substance Abuse	9
2	Unwanted Pregnancy	13
3	Unbelief in God	17
4	Social Engineering	21
5	Rising of the Occult	26
6	Bad Memories and Trauma	30
7	Lost Christian Home Life	34
8	Back Biting	39
9	Uncontrolled Passions	45
10	Rudeness	50
11	A Quarrelsome Spirit	53
12	Lack of Peace	57
13	Misunderstanding of the Origin of Truth	60
14	Forgetting about Judgement Day	64
15	Thinking we are Perfect	67
16	The Goal of Barely Making it to Heaven	71
17	The Notion that Everyone is Going to Heaven	75
18	The Belief that Heaven is on Earth	79
19	Loss in the Belief in Purgatory	82
20	Love of Money, Power and Pleasure	86
21	Unjust Accusations	90
22	Believing we are like Animals	93
23	Too Few People Truly Know God	96
24	Lack of Happiness	99
25	Sins Against the First Commandment	103
26	Materialism	106
27	Pornography	111
28	Lack of Devotion	117
29	Imprudent Recreation	122
30	The Evil of the World Seems too Great to Overcome	127
31	The Scandal of the Catholic Church	131
32	Mistaken View of Virtue in our Times	135

Chapter One

Problem   SUBSTANCE ABUSE

Solution   TEMPERANCE

    It was a dry, sunny, and dusty day when the Sheriff's deputy of Maricopa County, where the city of Phoenix is located, led me to the men in jail. This was no ordinary jail. It was nicknamed Tent City because the men slept in tents. He took me to one of the open-walled tents hoping that I would "preach" to the inmates. I found a bunk and sat in it. Three men across from me stopped what they were doing and sat upright and gave attention. I was uncomfortable and unsure how God wanted to use me in this situation so I prayed a Hail Mary. Then I asked the fifty-year-old man in front of me, "What is your story?"

    Other men from the tent gathered around us.

    "Drugs brought me here," the man said. "In fact, Father, I think all of us are here because of drugs."

    As I stood up and began to speak, I noticed other men filing in from the surrounding tents.

    "We are all fighting a very difficult spiritual battle in our souls," I told them. "When the world, the flesh, or the devil presents us with temptation, we cannot give in. Men act effeminately when they give in to the triple source of sin. Drugs are very prevalent, and the devil uses them to get people into his grips. Men, we need to rise up and be manly when confronted by sin. The word *virtue* has the Latin word 'vir' as the root, which means 'man.' When confronted with evil we need to be manly."

More and more men were gathering for the sermon. And then I realized that I, in effect, called these men effeminate. The man in front of me had biceps ten times bigger than mine, but I continued. "All of you can get out of drug abuse and out of the life of jail by a life of prayer – the Holy Sacrifice of the Mass and the Rosary." I pulled out a Rosary. "This can help you the next time you are confronted with drug abuse."

I looked around and saw the men were a captive audience, but it came time to leave. I asked the Deputy Sheriff if we could leave. As we left, several of the men came up to me to shake my hand, and I gave them my blessing.

The Church has the answer to drug abuse. It is the acquisition of the virtue of temperance. St. Thomas distinguishes temperance generally and specifically. Temperance in general is moderation guided by reason to human operations and passions and is common to every moral virtue. Temperance specifically is different than fortitude, since temperance withdraws man from things which seduce the appetite from obeying reason.[1]

With regards to drug abuse, St. Thomas distinguishes a particular vice against temperance. In his times, it was drunkenness. He explains how drunkenness might not be a sin if someone drinks something but does not know that it contains alcohol and yet gets drunk.[2] It is a mortal sin to drink to get drunk on purpose if one has all three requirements for mortal sin, namely grave matter, full knowledge, and full consent. Sin causes death. "For the wages of sin is death, but the free gift of God is eternal life in Christ Jesus the Lord."[3]

So knowing is half the battle. How does one gain temperance to combat drug abuse? The spiritual life is very simple. Ask. Our Lord Jesus Christ told us, "Ask and it will be given you; seek, and you will find; knock, and it will be opened to you."[4] First, ask for the grace of repentance. Then ask for the virtue of temperance. Lastly, ask the Holy Spirit for the gift of temperance.

---

1 ST, Pt. II-II, Q. 141, Art. 2.
2 ST, Pt. II-II, Q. 150, Art. 1 & 2.
3 Romans vi: 23.
4 Matthew vii: 7.

For a Catholic, go to the Sacrament of Confession, attend Mass often, and receive Communion in the state of grace.

For all, pray the Rosary asking for the virtue of temperance. Wear a blessed Miraculous Medal. Wake up every morning and get down on your knees to consecrate every moment to God so the devil has none of it. When the temptation to use comes, say the name of Jesus and Mary over and over. Ask, in your heart, Jesus and Mary and the court of Saints for help in your own words. Make a Spiritual Communion. Ask for the blessing of a priest.

When I was a pastor, in my last weeks, two Catholic drug addicts died from drug abuse. I knew that I needed to go out into the streets and teach people how to overcome drug abuse before it was too late. The grip of drug abuse strengthens as time goes on, but when one gives generously to God, many gifts of conversion and reversion can come at an instant or over a long period of time.

If we are trying to help someone overcome drug addiction, we can start by saying a decade of the Rosary with them, asking for the virtue of temperance. If they do not want to pray it with you, pray for them to have the temperance to overcome the addiction.

I wonder if my "sermon" helped any of those men in the tent city? I conclude with a story of a homeless man in St. Joseph. After I helped serve the dinner at the St. Joseph Haven homeless shelter for men, a young man asked, "Father, will you give me a blessing that I can find a job?" I gave it to him and left.

About a year later, a St. Joseph City truck parked on the sidewalk and out came a young man in white shirt, tie, and formal trousers saying, "Father do you remember me?" I said, "I am trying." He said, "You gave me the blessing, and my life changed after that. That week I got a temporary job. Then I got a part-time job. Then I got a full-time job with the city, and later I was promoted to foreman with full health benefits. I want to thank you for that blessing."

I gave him a Rosary and a Miraculous Medal and told him to stop me whenever he sees me again so that we can catch up, and to wave or honk so I can give him another blessing. He holds true to what I asked him to do. I do not know if he was homeless due to drug abuse. But what I do know is that he asked God for help by asking for my priestly blessing, and then he did something positive, getting work. Later, I met him and he prayed a decade of the Rosary with me. He had a fierce determination to get out of his homeless situation. If a drug addict has that attitude, then he too can get out of his addiction by the graces of the God that come through prayer, the Mass, Communion, the Rosary, the Miraculous Medal, and the blessing of a priest.

Chapter Two

Problem UNWANTED PREGNANCY

Solution CHASTITY, PURITY, CONTINENCE, MODESTY AND REFINEMENT

I was walking as usual, praying my Rosary in a southern United States city when a couple caught my attention, "Father, are you for real?"

I looked at them and waited for them to approach. The young man mentioned that he liked the idea of a priest walking around the city. He told me his problems, gave me a $20 bill, and introduced me to his girlfriend. I gave them my card and encouraged them to call me before the end of the week as my mission would go back north.

Soon after, I got an email from the woman, thanking me for listening and giving her a Rosary and a blessing. I replied and asked if there were a coffee shop where we could meet. She agreed.

"What is your story?" I asked as we sat down. She told me about her spiritual life, crying through most of it, saying, "I had several abortions."

I encouraged her. "You are one of God's children, and He will forgive you if you repent from your sinful life and become a virtuous woman."

She thanked me for listening, noting that she had no one to talk to about these things.

The Christian drama is one where some souls go to eternal Hell, and some souls go to eternal Heaven and bliss. The main antagonist of the soul is the devil. He hates God and our human family because he does not want any human to take the empty throne he lost in heaven. He has done his work of changing culture from one that considered good good and evil evil to a culture that now considers good evil and evil good. So many members of our human family suffer from a culture influenced by the devil and humans choosing so much sin. The devil tempts us with half-truths, knowing that a bold lie will not work. But "he has nothing to do with the truth, because there is not truth in him..."[5] So in fraternal charity, a great love of each member of our human family, the Church has the answer to teenage pregnancy.

St. Thomas distinguishes the parts of the virtue of temperance needed. These virtues are needed to prevent actions that lead to pregnancy out of wedlock and the end result of abortion. The first one is chastity. "I answer that, Chastity takes its name from the fact that reason *chastises* concupiscence, which, like a child, needs curbing...Now the essence of human virtue consists in being something moderated by reason."[6] Concupiscence signifies those passions that move us to procreation. In themselves they are not wrong. Outside of the context of a lawfully married man and woman, sexual thoughts, words, and deeds are always wrong. The virtue of chastity helps curb the passions of procreation when they are not between a lawfully married man and woman.

The second part of temperance with regards to teenage pregnancy is purity. Purity is that virtue whereby one curbs "... for instance kissing, touching, and fondling."[7] Many teenagers have asked me in the past, "How far is too far?" The answer is *nada*, Spanish for "nothing." It is never a good idea to play with fire. Foreplay is only for a man and a woman who are lawfully married.

The third part of temperance with regards to teenage pregnancy is continence. Now some define continence as the virtue

---
5 St. John xiii: 44.
6 ST, Pt. II-II, Q. 151, Art. 1.
7 ST, Pt. II-II, Q. 143, Art. 1.

found in priests and the religious to never engage in thoughts, words, or deeds regarding procreation for their entire life. But St. Thomas wishes to use the word more generally in Part Two of Two in the *Summa Theologica*. Continence is the virtue found in the will "...when stirred by the impulse of passion: and this movement is restrained by *continence*, the effect of which is that, although a man suffer immoderate concupiscence, his will does not succumb to them."[8] This means that when the world, the devil, or our own self present temptations of the flesh in our imagination, words, or deeds, we choose good and avoid evil in our will. We do not entertain the temptation.

The fourth part of temperance with regards to teenage pregnancy is modesty. Modesty is that virtue that restrains "bodily movements and actions to moderation and restraint."[9] This means not walking around like a prostitute or wearing clothing that does not cover enough of the body.

The fifth part of temperance with regards to teenage pregnancy is refinement. Refinement is that virtue where "...a man observes decorum in what he does..."[10] In the height of Christendom, society in Europe was Catholic, and there was a certain God-fearing culture that practiced a decorum, a behavior keeping in good taste and propriety and etiquette that held up to the standards of God.

So how does one who has not lived these virtues begin? Or how does a parent instill these virtues into a child? Or how does one pray for a niece who does not have these virtues? Well, the Church has all the answers to our problems.

In general, one must decide to do what God wants. We should only say the Lord's Prayer if we only do what God wants. So one who has had teenage pregnancy should seek what God wants. End all relationships that prevent what God wants.

After this, a non-Catholic has many ways to be good after teenage pregnancy. First, learn to pray the Rosary and ask for the five virtues, one for each decade: chastity, purity, continence, modesty and refinement. Go and ask a priest for his priestly

---
8 ST, Pt. II-II, Q. 143, Art. 1.
9 ST, Pt. II-II, Q. 143, Art. 1.
10 ST, Pt. II-II, Q. 143, Art. 1.

blessing. Attend the Holy Sacrifice of the Mass without presenting oneself for Holy Communion. Ask others to pray for you to have these five virtues. Wear the Miraculous Medal and ask for these virtues on waking, and kiss the medal saying this prayer: "O Mary conceived without sin, pray for us who have recourse to thee." Buy a chastity ring and ask a priest to bless it. Consecrate yourself to the Blessed Virgin Mary as her slave, and ask her for the grace to start a life with the five virtues. Make spiritual Communions.

A Catholic can do all the above but also receive the Sacrament of Confession by examining her conscience and confessing all known mortal sins with contrition or attrition and doing the penance assigned by the priest. She can also go to Mass and receive Communion after she has made this Confession.

Relatives can pray Rosaries for their loved ones, begging God for the five virtues.

So, about that woman who poured out her heart to me in the southern city, I went back there a year later and met her on a city bench and caught up with her life. At the end of our conversation I asked, "Would you like to go to a sung Mass with me this evening?" She said, "Yes."

After Mass I asked, "How did it go?" She told me that she cried through most of it. Our Lord Jesus Christ came to visit this soul, the product of an evil society, and presented her with hope and a new life.

Chapter Three

Problem UNBELIEF IN GOD

Solution ASKING FOR THE GIFT OF FAITH

It was a cold, windy day, and I was walking in the stockyards of Saint Joseph, Missouri in 2017. A beat-up car stopped on the other side of the highway. The driver rolled down the window and asked, "Do you need a ride?" I said, "No," and traced the sign-of-the-cross over her and her two daughters.

She drove down the road, made a U-turn, and drove up to me again. She rolled down the window, and we greeted each other. I said, "Do you need some Rosaries?" She said that she did. After letting the girls pick out several Rosaries and giving them Miraculous Medals to wear, the 34-year-old woman told me her life story, which included stints in and out of jail, baptism by her parents because they did not remember if she was baptized at the local Catholic parish, many bad decisions, and four children out of wedlock. Her name was Sandra.

After she asked why I walk the streets, I told her how people are leaving the Church and do not come back anymore, so I need to go out into the streets. I told her, at my particular judgment, when Jesus asks what I did for him, I hope to say, "I encouraged Sandra and her two daughters to come to Your Holy Altars and receive your Body."

Sandra went on to explain that she did not think she could take her children to the Catholic Mass because they would be a distraction. I gave her my card with my name, phone, and email and told her my address. Then I blessed them, and I continued my walk.

Every year I meet hundreds of people like Sandra. They are curious about what I do, and I speak from my heart to theirs about how we live and die and are judged to Hell or Heaven for eternity. After I tell them how to find the path to salvation in the Church Jesus founded, the simple thing would be to follow the steps. But in reality, so few people go in that direction. Sin causes our life to become complicated. Sin causes us to give excuses why we should not follow the path that leads to Jesus Christ and our eternal salvation. Sandra had an excuse for every invitation that I gave her. For example, she indicated she could not take her children to Mass because they would interrupt. This and thousands of excuses are from the type of human family we have on earth. What is the problem? What is the remedy?

The problem is unbelief in general. The Church founded by Jesus Christ was created to make Him known and served in this life and in the next. In the 20th century, She has abandoned the missionary zeal of times past. Priests and Bishops used to walk into countries and propagate the Faith to unbelievers, but it seems the Church is too often ignoring this mandate from the very authority of Our Lord Jesus Christ. "Go out to the highways and hedges, and compel people to come in, that my house may be filled."[11] Even the teaching to the faithful seems to be all but completely abandoned. I meet so many fallen-away Catholics and children of fallen-away Catholics who have had poor catechesis, if any at all. It is so distressing. So what is the result? Unbelief is the greatest sin, and our whole human family is responsible for it.

St. Thomas asks the question "Whether unbelief is the greatest of sins? ...infidelity, is the sin to which all others may be traced. Therefore, unbelief is the greatest of sins."

He continues, "Every sin consists formally in aversion from God...Hence the more a sin severs man from God, the graver it is. Now man is more than ever separated from God by unbelief, because he has not even true knowledge of God: and by false

---

11 St. Luke xiv: 24.

knowledge of God, man does not approach Him, but is severed from Him."[12]

With the problem stated, "unbelief is the greatest of sins," what is the remedy? There are many ways to answer this question. In my observation the two best remedies are first, ask for the gift of faith. Second, do acts of charity.

Asking for the gift of faith is simple. Do not ask just with lip service, but from the heart! One must ask God for the gift of faith every day, never giving up. Learn how to say the Rosary and ask for the gift of faith before each Hail Mary and Our Father. Wear the Miraculous Medal and ask for the gift of faith every morning by kissing it and saying the prayer, "Oh Mary conceived without sin, pray for us who have recourse to thee." Read the Bible.

Do acts of charity. Fr. Garrigou-Lagrange relates a story of "...a young Jew, the son of a Vienna banker, one day had an opportunity to take vengeance on his family's greatest enemy: as he was about to do so, he remembered the following words of Scripture, which he was in the habit of reading from time to time: 'Forgive us our trespasses, as we forgive those who trespass against us.' Then instead of taking vengeance he fully pardoned his enemy and immediately received the gift of faith. He believed in the entire Gospel, and a short time afterward entered the Church and became a priest and religious. The precept of fraternal charity had illumined him."[13]

In Catholic Countries of centuries ago, it was common to have religious monasteries, convents, and abbeys in virtually every decent-sized town. I even remember reading a report where almost every hill was dotted with religious houses somewhere in Europe. These religious communities, when living up to their ideals, interceded for the common people. These nuns and monks interceded for the gift of faith for people.

I told the nuns at the convent where I am a chaplain the story of how I encountered Sandra on the highway, and I begged them to intercede for her to have faith. Whenever I encounter

---

12 ST, Pt. II-II, Q. 10, Art. 3.
13 Fr. Garrigou-Lagrange, *The Three Ages of the Interior Life*, vol. II, p. 202, Tan Books, Rockford, Illinois, 1989.

people who do not have the gift of faith, I ask the nuns to pray for them. In spiritual combat, God can give our human family help. God only works through our free will and he will help the Sandras of the world, if our human family, including religious, beg Him. As it was said earlier, there was a time when monasteries dotted the hills. We need that again.

Chapter Four

Problem SOCIAL ENGINEERING AIMED AT THE DESTRUCTION OF THE KINGDOM OF GOD

Solution DEVOTION TO THE HOLY FACE OF JESUS

The first time I walked *el Camino de Santiago de Campostela*, or the Way of St. James in Spain, I met an interesting middle-aged woman. For several days she poured out her heart of her spiritual journey to me, as many souls do since I am a priest. In short, she grew up Catholic but began to forget her religious heritage. In her later teen years, she became a foreign exchange student, living with a Protestant family in the United States. She marveled at the fervor of her host family in their religious observance. Eventually she decided to join that particular sect and sought to evangelize in her home country of Spain with this particular observance of Protestantism. She told me, "Father, the Catholic Faith in Spain is dead." In my observation, I think she was right.

There are many reasons for the demise of the Catholic faith in Spain. One of them includes the Spanish Civil war. In the 1930s, revolutionary men began a civil war between fascism and democracy in Spain. At the beginning of the war fifty-one Claretian Brothers were martyred for wearing the cassock. "On July 20, 1936, some sixty anarchists or 'minute men' broke into the gate house of the missionaries.[14] Two rifleman, under orders from the revolutionary 'Committee,' rounded everyone up and had them stand in ranks."[15] After several days these men studying to become perpetually professed as brothers and some to go forward to become priests were martyred at gunpoint several days after imprisonment. Historians and authors called these anarchists various and sundry names from Fascists to Communists to Revolutionary men. The point is that there are revolutionary men who have chosen to revolt against God. This revolution is led by sinful men, and they attack the Catholic Culture and Her priests, families and even children unborn in the womb. The enemies of God use these men to change a God-fearing culture to an evil and perverse culture as Our Lord Jesus Christ dealt with in his public ministry. "O faithless and perverse generation..."[16] These revolutionary men are living among us today, and they are bent on destroying our Catholic heritage. One of their methods is social engineering. "Socialists, Communists and Nihilists...strive to uproot the foundations of civilized society."[17] Social engineering is the use of social media like television, radio, internet, etc. to uproot the foundations of civilized society by using various means like propaganda and pornography, to name a few, to attack the Catholic Church. My Spanish friend on the Camino said, "The Catholic Faith in Spain is dead," and I think this is partially the result of revolutionary men and their use of social engineering.

Notice that technology is one of the chief means to uproot the foundations of civilized society. Technology in itself is good and can be used to provide the means of teaching the faith and good morals. But it can also lead to immorality and mental illness. "...Because television provides a constant stream of images it is easy for a person to surrender volitional control of the imagination which is fed constant images and sound by television. This mechanism has a general pacifying effect, it makes the person passive. In order to watch television, there has to be a certain

---

14 Villeges, Gabriel Campo, Claretian Martyrs of Barbastro, Claretian Publications, 1992, p. 5.
15 Ibid, p. 6.
16 St. Matthew xvii: 17.
17 Pope Leo XIII, Quod apostolici muneris, (Dec. 28, 1878)

surrendering of the imagination to images provided by television. This can be dangerous in that one can just allow the television to do the thinking for him."[18] Thus revolutionary men can place immoral ideals in society by this means of social engineering. For example, we see this constantly in the attack on Christian femininity. An author mentioned a cartoon where Superwoman came in to help some men who were fighting some bad guys. This very attractive women in tight clothing swooped down to take care of business. The plot was to show that everyone had to look to the woman for help today as the new superman. This does not bring to light the beautiful work of a mother who stays at home, helps raise the children, and cooks nurturing meals. This is not teaching little girls how the hidden life of a housewife is fundamental for a civilized society.

Historically, the revolution has been going on since Adam and Eve. There was a time when Catholic Europe was at its strongest in the thirteenth century, and the Kingdom of God was gaining strength. But the revolution in sinful men broke out in the Protestant revolt at the beginning of the sixteenth century and has spread its tentacles to our modern times. In the middle of the nineteenth century, heaven intervened in a special way to a Carmelite nun in Tours, France, and eventually a long-time devotion, the Holy Face of Jesus, received the official status as an Archconfraternity in 1885 by Pope Leo XIII.

In the 1840s, Our Lord Jesus Christ privately revealed to Sister Mary of Saint Peter that He desires an Association formed and named Defenders of the Holy Name of God, an army of valiant soldiers uniting themselves to Him as to their 'Commander-in-Chief.' This association properly approved and organized by Pope Leo XIII has a twofold purpose; first, reparation for blasphemy and second, reparation for the profanation of Sundays and Holy Days of obligation. On October 4, 1846 Sister Mary of Saint Peter wrote, "Our Lord communicated to me that this time He would use as the instruments of punishment, not the elements, but "the malice of revolutionary men."[19] Even if these private revelations

---

18 Fr. Ripperger, Chad, Ph. D, Introduction to the Science of Mental Health, Vol. 1: Philosophical Psycology, 2001, Chad Ripperger, p. 280.
19 Sister Mary of St. Peter, The Golden Arrow, Tan Publishers, Rockford, Il. 1990, p. 177.

are not proven to be true, it is safe to observe that social engineering is driving the collapse of civilized society along with our human family's growing sinfulness.

So in a word, it does not take a Doctorate degree in Theology to see that our culture continues to spiral into self-destruction. There are many ways to mount a counter-revolt, and one of them is clearly given in the devotions to the Holy Face of Jesus. Our human family has sinned most gravely in the first of the Commandments,[20] which are attacks directly onto God Himself, the Most Holy Trinity. The later Commandments deal with justice due to our neighbor. Sins of the flesh, for example, are sins of weakness and do not attack the Face of God directly, yet they are still mortal wounds to the soul. But blaspheming His Most Holy Name and not giving Him the minimum worship that is due to Him is a direct attack on Him. God, in His justice, eventually gives our human family what we want, sin, and the fruits of our sin. His worst punishment is not earthquakes or tempests, but the malice of 'revolutionary men.' So how to do we mount a counter-revolt against these revolutionary men?

Find a Confraternity of the Most Holy Face of Jesus and make reparation for the sins of our human family. This will appease the wrath of God and begin to help you. The following prayer was revealed by Our Lord to Sister Mary of Saint Peter of Tours in 1843 as a reparation for blasphemy. "This Golden Arrow will wound My Heart delightfully," He said, "and heal the wounds inflicted by blasphemy."

> The Golden Arrow
> May the most holy, most sacred, most adorable, most incomprehensible and ineffable Name of God, be forever praised, blessed, loved adored and glorified, in heaven, on earth, and in the hells, by all the creatures of God, and by the Sacred Heart of Our Lord Jesus Christ in the most Holy Sacrament of the Altar. Amen.[21]

---

20 The first three Commandments deal with sins directly against God Himself.
21 Imprimatur: +T. K. Gorman, D.D., Bishop of Dallas-F. Worth; Nihil obstat: C. L. Mulholland, Censo Librorum, Feb. 29, 1956. This prayer is popularly found in the booklet called the Pieta Prayer Book.

Making reparation for blasphemy and profanation of Sundays and Holy Days is one important step to mount a counter-revolution to the ungodly revolution. Another step is removing the propaganda from our own homes. "...but as for me and my house, we will serve the Lord."[22] We must remove the anathema, the thing devoted to evil, the accursed thing in order to mount a victorious counterattack in our own Christian homes. The restoration of Christian culture requires us to "...smash the television set. The Catholic Church is not opposed to violence; only to unjust violence, so smash the television set."[23] It is time to bring back Christian chivalry and spiritual competition. All the sports that we watch arouse a spirit of competition with their winners and losers, but it is an artificial sport that removes us from the valiant sport of Christian warfare where the winners receive the victory of heaven and the losers the punishment of hell, each respectively for eternity! May souls rise up above this present-day adversity like eagles and engage in the battle of all battles for our very salvation!

So what is the rest of the story of my Catholic friend in Spain? She had the grace to go to a good priest who helped her discern her way back home to the Catholic Church. She considered religious life, but after trying her vocation in religion, has remained single. She posed an exciting endeavor to myself and John, my *Camino* buddy. "Come to my home city of Valencia to see the Holy Grail." So after the *Camino* we booked a train to Valencia and saw the holy chalice that very likely was used by Our Lord Jesus Christ at the Last Supper.

---

22 Joshua xxiv: 15.
23 Dr. John Senior, The Restoration of Christian Culture, IHS Press, Norfolk, VA, 2008, p. 22.

Chapter Five

Problem   RISING OF THE OCCULT
Solution   STUDIOUSNESS

It was a hot, sunny day in St. Joseph, Missouri, as I was walking in the worst part of town one afternoon. A woman looked at me and asked, "Aren't you hot in that outfit?" I explained that it was good for me to be mortified and to suffer for Our Lord Jesus Christ. She then said, "Put that cross away, it is too bright! But I want to see that thing on your left hand." She was referring to the Rosary. I replied, "No one is going to tell me to stop carrying this Crucifix around. I am proclaiming the death of Our Lord Jesus Christ, and I am praying to the Blessed Virgin Mary to intercede for the conversion and reversion of all that live in St. Joseph." Then I asked, "What is your name?" She replied, "I do not have a name. They call me 'Dragon Lady.'" I answered, "You need to have a Christian name. May I give you one?" She said, "No. I like my name. I am one of fifty children. My parents practice the occult." The bus arrived to pick her up, and I gave her my blessing.

    I have been a priest for over ten years and have observed the occult in every city that I have lived in, including small towns in Kansas, metropolises, and in St. Joseph, Missouri. It is an epidemic. There was a killing in a local park several years ago that was described in the local newspapers as an occult killing. The woman even said in court that if she were in charge of the killing, "There would have been no trace." They sacrificed a teenage girl because they needed the blood for one of their rituals.

After listening and reading the experiences of exorcists in our time, I observe that the demons are gradually leading our generations to greater malevolence. At first suffering was not dealt with. Then the next generation did not want their children to suffer, leading to a generation of irreligiosity and apostasy, to the current generation, giving birth to children, who generally sin grievously and without constraint against the sixth and ninth commandments, to the youngest generation, who are exploring outright demonic worship, chiefly by means of the internet.[24]

Many things are responsible for this corporate slide into the occult. Fr. Amorth, a former Roman exorcist, explains that "...a decline in faith life is directly connected to an increase in superstition."[25] So as we are humans endowed with both bodies and souls, we have both physical and spiritual needs. There is an inverse relationship between faith and superstition. When faith declines superstition increases. Superstition has been accelerated in our times by various and sundry factors like misuse of the internet and video games. One serious vice with regards to these objects is curiosity. Curiosity deals with the desire and study in the pursuit of knowledge, which in itself is not bad. But, the desire to study knowledge can be bad, for example, "...when a man studies to learn of one, by whom it is unlawful to be taught, as in the case of those who seek to know the future through demons. This is superstitious curiosity..."[26] When someone is searching on the internet, the desire to know what is behind the next click, or the desire to get to the next stage in the video game can easily be used as a temptation by the demons to explore the occult and to be lead to greater and greater vice. Someone begins to study in order to know a truth above the capacity of his own intelligence, since by so doing men easily fall into error.[27] It is dangerous when individuals research the occult without the necessary knowledge

---

24 Fr. Ripperger, Chad, Latin Mass Magazine, "The Sixth Generation," Summer 2012, pp. 34-38.
25 Fr. Amorth, Gabrielle, An Exorcist More Stories, Ignatius Press, San Francisco, 2012, p. 63.
26 ST, Pt. II-II, Q. 167, A. 1.
27 Ibid.

of theology on the internet. When a soul slips from one sin to a worse sin repeatedly, over time he sins against the most important commandments, one through three. The demons lead them from disobedience to parents, to sins of the flesh, to outright demonic worship. So where do we go from here?

I will be forever grateful to my father, who did not allow us to buy an upgrade from Atari video games to Nintendo in the 1980s. He told us to go play outside. This developed into gathering young men from the neighborhood and playing baseball during our summers. We engaged ourselves in physical activity and used our minds to be creative and learn how to deal with people face to face, and not in a virtual world. Those summer days gave me experiences and good desires that led me to the priesthood and the desire to walk around saving souls like Our Lord Jesus did. These experiences helped me begin to desire a certain excellence and leadership skills. By this desire of excellence, I was interested in a life of virtue, doing good, and avoiding evil. One of these virtues was studiousness.

St. Thomas explains the virtue of studiousness as applying the mind to something in an ordered way, as opposed to the vice of neglect of study, and the excess, namely curiosity.[28] St. Augustine says, "We are forbidden to be curious: and this is a great gift that temperance bestows."[29]

As the world continues to rely more and more on technology, the vices wrapped up in misuse of it will become stronger. It is important to form our human family in studiousness so that we have virtues to combat the vices of curiosity. We do well to moderate our use of the internet and video games. Recreation is an art and 're-creates' us to become more wholesome in our everyday lives and should lead us to a greater relationship with God. Parents should prevent or regulate use of social media for their children, so they may develop the virtues needed to moderate use of social media in the future, when the temptations of curiosity arise. A life of prayer and partaking of the sacraments of Holy Mother Church are the surest ways to combat vice and the ever-growing strength of the occult. The Church has all the answers in

---

28 ST, II-II, Q. 166, A. 2.
29 De Morib. Eccl. 21.

any age because the wisdom and very authority of Our Lord Jesus Christ are given to us by the Church down through the ages.

What ever happened to 'Dragon-Lady'? I have not seen her again. My encounter makes me think of the dark world of the occult that is growing around us. The Church is the answer to the problem of the occult. The Church has the power to change the culture. There is nothing to be afraid of if we turn our gaze to Our Lord Jesus Christ and the Blessed Virgin Mary. "...She shall crush thy head, and thou shall lie in wait for her heal."[30]

These are the words of God after the serpent deceived Adam and Eve. The serpent was made to crawl on the ground and be tied to us humans, eating dust all the days. The Blessed Virgin Mary is the instrument to crush the serpent. The humble Mary shall crush the proud serpent.

---

30 Gen. iii: 15.

Chapter Six

Problem BAD MEMORIES LEADING TO MENTAL ILLNESS

Solution DISCUSSION AND PRAYER LED BY THE VIRTUE OF PRUDENCE

As I was nearing home one afternoon in St. Joseph, a man in his 60's with signs of alcohol abuse approached me on the corner and challenged me. "You shouldn't walk around here. You're going to get hurt." I remarked, "I have been walking here over a year and have never had a problem." He looked at my Crucifix and said, "Put that away. Nobody wants you walking around here with that." I answered, "Everyone needs Jesus around here. I am going to keep going." After I gave him my blessing, I smiled.

Several months later, I happened to walk by his house. He heckled me again, so I gave him another blessing, smiled, and kept walking.

A couple of months after that I walked in front of his house and he called me over. He said, "I know that you are nice. Do you want a cigarette?" After telling him that I am not a smoker, he told me his story. I found out that he drank all the time primarily because he was angry that God took his five-year-old son. Every time that his memory brought this to mind, he acted out by drinking it away.

Mental illness can result with the imprudent use of our memory. Some may experience great emotional pain and alter the actual experience in their mind. For example, someone might be falsely accused of harming a child, when they never did that. The public humiliation might be so emotionally painful that one might think that he did harm the child, when in fact he never did. The memory needs to be reformulated so that only what indeed did happen is recalled. Sometimes an experience is so bad that the emotional pain causes malfunctioning of other faculties. For example, when one is standing up publicly for the truth of Our Lord Jesus Christ, a disgruntled person may send an anonymous letter stating the lie that "everyone is up in arms with what you said," when actually only a few people are disgruntled because they have been presented with a truth of Our Lord Jesus Christ, and now this small group is challenged to reform their lives to continue to be considered Christian. The one who stood up for the rights of Our Lord Jesus Christ, assuming all the necessary virtues were present, including prudence, may be so hurt that he stops presenting the truth. If he continues to recall this emotional pain, it can be detrimental, leading to emotional illness like paranoia, to name one example. It is like being wounded by a knife in the heart. The wound is originated by one who wrote the anonymous letter, but every time the memory is used to bring up that wound, it is like taking the knife and moving it around. The memory continues to open the scab. So what is the remedy?

St. Thomas speaks about the eight integral parts of the virtue of prudence.[31] And Bl. Francisco Palau, using the source of St. Thomas, lists them accordingly: "memory, reasoning, intelligence-understanding, docility, solicitude, providence, discretion, vigilance."[32] It serves us well to be prudent in all we do by doing the right thing, at the right time, and in the right way. Our memories are used by prudence to accomplish things in the best way by using right reason and recalling things that are good for us and are accurate. But sometimes our memories can be unhealthy from physical injury or from past emotional wounds, like someone putting a knife in our heart. We deal with the later, interior sense.

---
31 ST, Pt. II-II, Q. 48, A. 1.
32 Bl. Francisco Palau, Writings, Editorio Monte Carmelo, 2006, Burgos, Spain.

"Sometimes memory can be healed by discussing it and merely flushing out the past memory."[33] In other words, after talking about it to a competent person, first forget about the past hurt, stop moving the knife around. Then, secondly, pray for the healing of the memory. When the bad memory arises, offer it to the hands of the Blessed Virgin Mary and ask her to put it into her Immaculate Heart. St. Anthony Mary Claret "...understood Mary's Immaculate Heart to be a new Noah's ark. By entering her heart, mankind would be able to find a place of safety against the spiritual deluge overtaking the world."[34] We should ask the Blessed Virgin Mary to love our enemies through her Immaculate Heart, through her motherhood. Every time a wound comes up in the memory, we need to make this offering. Our Lord Jesus Christ said, "...unless you be converted and become as little children, you shall not enter into the kingdom of heaven."[35] So we do well to understand that these memories are so difficult to take care of ourselves, and we adopt the childlike spirituality and turn to our Mother with these or similar words, "Dear Mary, I cannot deal with this, '...I am worm, and no man: the reproach of men and the outcast of people.'[36] I simply put this hurt into your hands and let you take care of it as our Mother, given that I do my duty." Then we can ask for the union of the Sacred Heart of Jesus and the Immaculate Heart of Mary. "It is not sufficient to look upon our neighbor benevolently; we must love him effectively. We can do this by bearing with his defects, returning good for evil, avoiding jealously, and praying for the union of hearts."[37] A life of intense prayer helps the soul to receive the inspirations from the Sacred Heart of Jesus and the Immaculate Heart of Mary how to deal

---

[33] Fr. Ripperger, Chad, Ph. D., Introduction to the Science of Mental Health, Vol. 1: Philosophical Psychology, 2001, Chad Ripperger, p. 294.
[34] Calloway, Donald H, MIC, Champions of the Rosary: The History and Heroes of a Spiritual Weapon, Marian Press, Stockbridge, MA, 2016, p. 222.
[35] St. Matthew xviii: 3.
[36] Psalm xxi: 7.
[37] Fr. Garrigou-Lagrange, O.P., The Three Ages of the Interior Life: Prelude to Eternal Life, Vol. II, Tan Books and Publishers, Rockford, Illinois, 1989, p. 210, section on Fraternal Charity.

with each person in our lives, friend or foe. Our Lord Jesus said, "...pray for them that persecute and calumniate you."[38] One of the signs of a soul advancing in the spiritual life is one who can truly pray for his enemies.

One of the quickest and surest means of achieving a true prayer life for those who hurt us and to forgive those who trespass against us is to make the Total Consecration to the Blessed Virgin Mary, according to the method of St. Louis de Montfort.

What ever happened to the angry man? After he revealed his anger to God for the death of his son, I understood part of why he abused alcohol. Every time he thought of his little child, he attributed his anger towards God. He drank to forget about it, and drinking to excess as he did comes with many more problems. As Christians, we ask God to give us Faith, so we can know how the providence of God is good, how His grace is sufficient for each trial, and how to lead a life of goodness in the truth. After encouraging him with the right response to his loss and giving him the Rosary to pray, I took my leave. I have not heard from him yet, but next time I hope to pray a decade of the Rosary with him, focusing on the Fifth Sorrowful Mystery, the Crucifixion.

---

38 St. Matthew v: 44.

Chapter Seven

Problem　LOST CHRISTIAN HOME LIFE

Solution　THE BENEDICT OPTION OR
　　　　　　THE AUGUSTINIAN OPTION

As a priest, I am a spiritual father to the masses of peoples. I get invited to the home and have the intimate experience of how each family lives behind their doors. One time I was giving instructions to a father, who I met on the streets while walking. He was inquiring about becoming Catholic. As I entered the house, the television was blaring, the computers were on, and the children brought their cell phones with their loud video games to show us every few minutes. It was difficult, to say the least, to convey some spiritual and theological points when the span of concentration was interrupted every two minutes.

I once heard on the radio, "The family that prays together, stays together." In these modern times the family is attacked on all sides. Revolutionary men are used by the kingdom of Satan to divide the family home. Most do not even know that it is important to put up a fight because the revolution against God has taken ground each generation slowly but surely, so children have learned from their parents in the home the vices the world has to offer, namely video games and television. "Today the home is often little more than a dreary place of transit where one sleeps and sometimes eats, devoid of common life."[39]

---

39 Fr. Bethel, Francis, O. S. B., John Senior and the Restoration of Realism, Thomas More College Press, 2016, p. 213.

In the culture wars, where the family is the battleground, one cannot be passive in the onslaught of secularism and humanism. One must return fire with intellectual warfare and entrust this battle to God, who wants our families to become strong and populate heaven. My family was strong, relatively speaking. We had meals in common and went on walks and picnics together, but the modern world of technology was also rooted in our home. I went to a monastery in Oklahoma called Our Lady of the Annunciation of Clear Creek Abbey when I was twenty-five. I remember it vividly. It was a Sunday evening. The sun was beginning to set as I went to the old horse stable, converted into a chapel topped with a little bell tower. I entered the tin building, the first place of worship before they built a church that should last one thousand years. The incense was so thick I could barely see the walls. I saw about fifteen monks moving around with a prayerful gravity, some kneeling on the concrete floor, some making a devotion to a statue here and one there, some praying the beads of the Rosary, and some clearing the Altar after Benediction. After several minutes, the bell rang, and a silence filled with grace descended upon my soul as the monks lined up in formation for Vespers. The organ gave an introduction, and I saw and heard Gregorian Chant live for the first time. "*Dixit Dominus Domino meo: Sede a dextris meis,*" "The Lord said to my Lord: Sit at My right hand."

At first, I was raised to the heavens and the sweetness of this experience soothed my soul, but then I was angry and thought to myself, "Why have I never seen this before? Why did I have to drive four hours to experience this beauty? This needs to be in a city!" A seed was planted.

How does this experience help cultivate the home life? Read further. "More than half the battle of life is already won when someone comes from a good family milieu."[40] In the restoration of culture, the arts, education, media, philosophy and music are family essentials. There are many ways that families can restore culture in their homes, but the scope of this book does not allow me to explore all the options. However, there are two that I hope to cover.

---

40 Ibid., p. 213.

When the surrounding culture is in darkness, a father and a mother can school themselves by reading good Catholic sources and implement Catholic culture in their homes wherever they may live. But this is difficult. There is the Benedict Option, where families move to a monastery in the country. If they live close enough, they may hear the bell and be reminded that the monks are going into spiritual battle for prayer to fulfill their vows and intercede for our human family. A child growing up around a monastery will not only learn by experience but will be able to live in an agrarian environment, a rural setting raising farm animals, camping and playing in the creeks and the woods. All this can help develop creative powers and a sense of awe and wonder simply by living in God's nature. A home that has music as its center instead of television will help children develop active skills instead the passive reception of television. "If you measure the hi-fi against the piano, for example, you can see that families don't gather around the stereo and sing. Families don't draw their chairs up closer to the central heating duct. No one sings while attending to the automatic dishwasher."[41]

The great thing about God is that there are many ways to live culture with God as the object. "Now there are a diversity of graces, but the same Spirit..."[42] Another option is the Augustinian option, where a monastery is set up in the city. St. Martin of Tours "...founded a community, the first in the city which was later to be illustrious with St. Ambrose and St. Augustine."[43] These were city monks who in the fourth century founded a type of community. "In the West, there was no monk who was not an apostle."[44] Although the rule of St. Martin's community is not extant, it can be built upon the rule of St. Augustine. Imagine the experience I had at the Benedictine monastery in the country, if it were in a city. With the help of God, it can be reproduced with its own culture. Imagine a

---

41 Dr. John Senior, *The Restoration of Christian Culture*, IHS Press, Norfolk, VA, 2008, p. 72.
42 1 Corinthians xii: 4.
43 Gheon, Henry, *St. Martin of Tours*, Sheed and Ward, New York, 1946, p. 33.
44 Ibid., p. 40.

Gothic church in the downtown area on a balmy day with the doors and stained-glass windows opened. The incense is so thick that it escapes the church. Chant can be heard by those who pass by on the sidewalk. If one is attracted to walk into the open doors, he would see city monks chanting and moving in the most beautiful theater and symphony of the world, the Church's gift of the Holy Sacrifice of the Mass and the Divine Office, or popularly known as Gregorian chant.

> "What we need for a sane Christian life together is a truly *noble* simplicity, the silence of anonymity, clouds of beautiful song and incense, a healthy routine of life marked by feasts and processions, a life of worship spent in churches that foster an ecstatic praise of God, bearing witness to his transcendent beauty...The traditional liturgy is thus the *chief missionary tool* of the Catholic Church, her main point of contact with the Jews, Muslims, Eastern Christians, Hindus, Africans, and so on."[45]

With the center of the lives of the city monks focused on God in the Divine Liturgies, families that live near the monastery will have the chance to participate in the ancient cottage industries of pre-industrial revolution times, where both mother and father were in earshot every day, even at work. Learning the arts of leather making, silver smithing, honey making, carpentry, marble sculpting, chanting, winemaking, printing and a classical education, along with eating with the monks, can help a family form their children to become leaders in the future.

The Augustinian option lends itself to *ferens sacra in mundum*, or 'bringing the sacred into the world' using the sign-of-the-cross and the hundreds of sacramentals, like the Rosary, the Miraculous Medal, the Brown Scapular and the Holy Face, to bring souls to the holy altars of God.

The Church has answers to all the problems of the world.

---

45 Dr. Kwasniewski, Peter, Resurgent in the Midst of Chrisis: Sacred Liturgy, the Traditional Latin Mass, and Renewal in the Church, Angelico Press, Kettering, Ohio, 2014, pp. 152-153.

Since "faith cometh by hearing," it is easier for families to learn about the ways of God by the examples of monks. Watching the holy lives and living among them with all the proper boundaries, including cloister, can only aid in building the Kingdom of God here on earth. The Church has in mind, "to bring the riches of the Catholic faith, with all of its Tradition, more effectively in the world today; to spread the fragrance of Christ – His grace and truth – far and wide for the salvation of souls.

So what ever happened to that father who was inquiring about the Faith? He stopped attending classes, but I am hopeful that he will one day come back. If only there were some monks in the city so he could see them serving God daily, he might be drawn to come back to learn of God and enter into His Holy Church.

Chapter Eight

Problem   BACKBITING

Solution   JUSTICE

     Morally speaking, we are living in a cesspool of degradation. Even people that want to be good are clueless about the moral law of God. In my observation, many good priests who want to stand up for the rights of God have gone into parishes and gotten thrashed by the people there. These pastors have kept in mind the accounting of their particular judgment. I remember once a talk the Venerable Archbishop Fulton Sheen gave to priests, where he stated that we must make an accounting of every soul in our parish boundaries, whether they are practicing Catholics or pagans. As a bishop and once an Ordinary, having charge of all the people in a certain region in the state of New York, these words are even more onus for a Bishop. I have seen good priests and bishops who have had their reputation so besmirched from backbiting that their pastoral charge was rendered useless by the very sheep whom he was trying to save from the grip of Hell. Well, what are we to expect? The great High Priest, Our Lord Jesus Christ, suffered constantly, eventually subjected to the Passion and finally dying on a Cross. Evil tongues were the chief weapons used to murder the great High Priest, and they continue to murder the good name of bishops, priests, and everyone in our human family.

     One of the chief instruments to ruin the reputation of a person is by backbiting. "If a serpent bite in silence, he is nothing better that backbiteth."[46] The backbiter "...injures another by

---
46 Eccles. x. 11.

words...secretly by backbiting...injuring his good name."[47] In my observation, my generation, Generation X, suffers from a general defect of narcissism. This narcissism includes feeding our egos and pleasing people at all costs. Sometimes we please our peers by backbiting people we do not like or disagree with. Sometimes we listen to backbiting with delight. This feeds our pride and can be the ruin of our soul. This is backbiting. There is a book that helped me to understand the nature and prevalence and the evil of backbiting, *Sins of the Tongue: The Backbiting Tongue* by Father Belet, Diocese of Basle.

What is backbiting? "It is every sort of wicked word we dare not speak in front of a person about whom we are talking."[48] Father Belet points out eight types of backbiting to our neighbor:

1. Imputing things against his neighbor that never happened
2. When he brings a hidden or unknown fault to light, this is called detraction, defined as secret truths about a person that have no need to be uncovered.
3. Exaggeration
4. Relating something about neighbor that is not evil in any way, but speaking as though his neighbor had done it for evil reasons
5. Giving cold and reserved praise. Although our lips praise the person, our tone of voice and our body language indicate condemnation.
6. A simple gesture, raising the eyebrows, wagging his head
7. When asked about integrity or morals, or his neighbor is accused of some crime, he says nothing, even though it is known that he is virtuous or did not do the crime.
8. Finally, a person is guilty of backbiting if he is publicly blamed for something he did and he denies his guilt, thereby making his accuser pass for a liar.[49]

---

47 ST, Pt. II-II, Q. 73, Art. 1.
48 Fr. Belet, Sins of the Tongue: The Backbiting Tongue, Editions Magnificat, Mont-Tremblant, Quebec, Canada, 4th edition, 2006, p. 4.
49 Ibid., pp. 5-8.

Backbiting if done maliciously is a mortal sin. But it is a venial sin if it is done out of lightness of heart for some unnecessary motive, unless the word perchance is of grave nature and the cause of notable injury to a man's good name. One is bound to restore a man his good name...when treating of restitution.[50] And Scripture follows this sentiment. "Backbiters, hateful to God," which epithet, according to a gloss, is inserted, "lest it be deemed a slight sin because it consists in words."[51] Scripture depicts the tongue as fire, which does damage to one's good name. "What chastisements will be inflicted on you, O treacherous tongue? Sharp arrows of a warrior with fiery coal of brushwood."[52] "The tongue is a fire."[53] We do well to think of the tongue as a flame thrower on one's good name. Once a house goes up in fire, it is lost. It is easy to burn a house in less than a day, but it takes months to build it up again. Once our tongue destroys a good name, it can be done as rapidly as a bolt of lightning, and it may take months or even a lifetime to rebuild.

I remember reading a fictional story of one who confessed backbiting to a priest. The priest withheld absolution, commanding the penitent to go home, get a pillow, and return to the confessional, dropping feathers along the way. When the penitent confessed, the priest gave the penance to pick up the feathers. The penitent said, "The wind has blown them all over the four corners." The priest, making his point and giving a merciful penance, said, "And that is why you must keep these things in your throat, because once they slip out, there is no way to make them return. They run, they fly, they go on an endless journey."

How do we prevent backbiting? Pray the Rosary asking the Blessed Virgin Mary for the virtue of discretion, or circumspection, attending to the circumstances of the matter in hand. This means remaining silent and considering all the circumstances before speaking. "Let no evil speech proceed from

---

50 ST, Pt. II-II, Q. 73, Art. 2.
51 Rom. i: 30.
52 Ps cxix: 3.
53 Prov. xvi: 27

your mouth; but that which is good, to the edification of faith, that it may administer grace to the hearers."[54] If it is not good, don't say it, unless one has an office to correct out of charity or a duty to take counsel, deliberating how to prudently correct a sinner for his repentance and conversion. Sometimes remaining silent is the way of virtue, the way of discretion. We have two ears and one tongue. This discretion was religiously observed by the Blessed Virgin Mary. "Mary kept in mind all these things, pondering them in her heart."[55]

Beware of bad company, backbiters. Where two or three are gathered, there is the devil. Be careful the kind of friends you pick. You will become like them. When backbiters have no charity toward brother, their love of God is a lie.

How do we make restitution? It is the common principle among theologians, including St. Thomas and St. Augustine, that restoring their neighbor's reputation is obligatory. St. Thomas explains how to make restitution for one's good name. First, "When it is impossible to repay the equivalent, it suffices to repay what one can, as in the case of honor due to God and our parents. Second, there are three ways to take away one's good name:

1. Justly, saying what is true about one's sin, while observing right order. He is not bound to restitution.
2. By saying what is untrue and unjustly. He is bound to restitution by confessing that he told an untruth.
3. By saying what is true, but unjustly, when a man detracts by revealing a secret sin that is not required to reveal. He is bound to restore his good name as far as he possibly can.[56]

St. Vincent Ferrer was a remarkable preacher who had the gift of tongues. Namely, thousands of people would follow him around Europe and when he preached; everyone understood regardless of foreign language or dialect. Once words would leave the lips of the great preacher, they were translated mid-air by the

---
54 Eph. iv: 29.
55 Lk. ii: 51.
56 ST, Pt. II-II, Q. 62, Art. 2.

Holy Spirit in such a way that each hearer could understand in his own tongue. It was even reported that his voice boomed to the thousands of pilgrims, without aid of an amplifier, who followed him around Europe, centuries before the advent of electronic amplifiers. He also performed a little under ten thousand miracles. He had this to say about repairing our neighbor's reputation:

"The person who maliciously robs his neighbor's reputation is held to restoring it on the same level as someone who steals. If what you said is secret, even though it be true, you are obliged to restore his reputation. Otherwise you will not go to heaven."

Listening to backbiters is a sin. "Hedge in your ears with thorns," in Holy Scripture, "listen not to the wicked tongue, and make doors and bars to thy mouth."[57] How do we endure listening to backbiting? Change the subject or leave! There are two different groups of backbiters. "First, there are those who hear it reluctantly, not without certain pangs of conscience. These people are guilty of nothing; they even deserve a reward from God, especially if they express their disapproval with unmistakable hints.

"Others remain silent, however, letting no one see whether they agree or not with what is said."[58] These are guilty sometimes as much or more than the backbiter. Backbiting and listening to backbiting can be occasion for a mortal sin.[59] St. Jerome rightly observes, "Where there are no listeners, there are no backbiters: the combat will close for want of combatants."[60]

Backbiting is a sin against the virtue of justice. Since backbiting wounds or destroys one's good name, it is necessary to repair the wound or destruction, by restitution. Justice is defined as giving one his due. Each is due a good name, which is necessary to make it in society, to obtain gainful employment, the peace that comes with harmony in a community, and spiritual and emotional well-being. If we struggle with backbiting, praying for the virtue of justice, prudence, and discretion in our Rosaries is a sure remedy.

---

57 Sir xxviii: 28.
58 Fr. Belet, Sins of the Tongue: The Backbiting Tongue, Editions Magnificat, Mont-Tremblant, Quebec, Canada, 4th edition, 2006, pp. 64-65.
59 ST, II-II, Q. 73, Art. 4.
60 St. Jerome, Ad Celant.

The Church has all the answers to our problems. The reason why the Blessed Virgin Mary was filled with grace was partly due to her fervent desire of the coming of the promised Redeemer and her concern for everyone in our human family. She is the Immaculate Conception, and all things are restored through Our Lord Jesus Christ, who was born in her immaculate womb. We do well to entrust all our enemies, real or perceived, all those whom we are tempted to backbite, and all backbiters who speak to us, and most especially ourselves into her hands, begging her to put all of us in her Immaculate Heart, helping us to love each other through her maternity.

What have we learned about good pastors who are the victims of backbiting who are attacked by the sheep of a parish? We learn from the village of Lu, Italy. Under the direction of Msgr. Alesandro Canora, the mothers gathered often with a pious devotion to the Most Holy Sacrament of the Altar and prayed if it be the will of God that their sons become priests or brothers and their daughters become religious. This small village, numbering a few thousand inhabitants, came 323 vocations, half to the priesthood and the other to religious life. Sometimes, I wonder, did they never speak ill of a priest? Perhaps not even one member of that community ever gave into backbiting a priest, the anointed of God.

What is the moral of the story? Our Lord Jesus Christ instituted the priesthood and holy orders to restore to order in a holy way, the disorder of our world. We get what we deserve. If we do not pray for vocations, we will not get priests. If we pray for vocations, we will get priests, who will be living copies of Our Lord Jesus Christ, and if they are holy, will restore to order the chaos of our times. When we purge ourselves of backbiting, derision, and all sins of the tongue and pray for people for the gift of charity among the community, we will get a foretaste of heaven in our communities. "Our conversation is in heaven."[61] When will we receive the ardent fire of the Sacred Heart and the Immaculate Heart to love one another, and begin practicing the justice and charity that is found in heaven?

---

61 Philippians iii: 20.

Chapter Nine

Problem UNCONTROLLED PASSIONS
Solution UNDERSTANDING THE VIRTUE OF FASTING AND ABSTINENCE

At the age of 23, I remember going to a party one Friday night, the typical scene, young people getting drunk. I had lived in Lawrence, graduated from the University of Kansas and had been used to the bar scene for several years. Over time, I noticed how partying, getting drunk, drug use, and fornication was a dead-end road, or rather the road to Hell. But at this party, my life was to change forever! By the Providence of God, some young people were having a "Catholic Party" next door. They heard that my friends and I would be there, so they made an appearance and invited us over.

We entered their house. It was clean, beautiful, and quiet. We talked about God, Jesus, and religion. They introduced themselves as SALT, Single Adults Living the Truth. They were a counter-revolt to the revolution against God. Then and there, I knew my path was changed forever and rooted in God, for they practiced abstinence, fasting and prayer, interceding for other young adults in order that they might find their way out of the parties, the roads to Hell. We ultimately gathered at the perpetual adoration chapel at St. Francis of Assisi, Wichita, Kansas, at 2 o'clock every Saturday morning, the hour most of the bars closed, and prayed that young adults would see the drunken parties as a road to Hell and find, instead, the road to God. We had faith that the spiritual world was real and that abstinence from sleep to pray during the night could and would change some of these people at these moments of darkness, giving them the light of faith in their souls to see the two roads, the one to Hell, and the one to Heaven.

Uncontrolled passions are leading many people to Hell. Our Lady of Fatima showed the three children that many souls are going to hell for sins against the sixth and ninth Commandment. Uncontrolled passions lead us to the seven deadly sins, especially: gluttony, lust, and anger. Gluttony is eating to excess. Lust is an illicit desire for the pleasures pertaining to the 6th Commandment (i.e. adultery, fornication, etc.). Anger is a vice in which one does not moderate the passion of anger; an inordinate desire for vindication arising from immoderate sorrow at some offense. The virtue of temperance moderates the pleasures of touch and feelings and puts these passions back into the proper order.

In the beginning, Adam had the gift of integrity and all the passions were controlled, but Adam disobeyed God and lost many of the gifts, including integrity. He and his progeny now have concupiscence, where our passions are out of control. The passions need to be moderated by temperance. If the passions are not moderated by temperance, they will control us. We will constantly sin by drunkenness, sex, and anger.

Temperance has certain parts that moderate specific vices. Two of them are fasting and abstinence. Fasting is refraining from food in general. Abstinence is refraining from eating certain kinds of foods. Some disputed that fasting and abstinence are not virtues. St. Thomas, citing Scripture, reckons abstinence and fasting as virtues.[62]

The root of unhappiness in our modern human society is immoderate pleasure, or frenetic intemperance. We want to feel good now. But since these feelings are not moderated by good reason, they are sinful. "For the wages of sin is death..."[63] Our modern human family in general does not want to suffer at all. This is partially right, but it is partially wrong. Since suffering entered the world through sin, it is a part of our fallen nature,

---

62 ST, PT II-II, Q. 146, Art. 1 & Q. 147, Art. 1.
63 Rm. vi: 23.

and we are prone to death. We know that in "...God, all things work together unto the good...".[64] He makes good out of evil, the privation of what ought to be. Our fallen human nature means that all of us will suffer. But we should never suffer in vain. Suffering meritoriously helps us to moderate our passions.

We suffer well when we are contrite and mortified. Contrition means we are sorry for choosing evil and rejecting good. Contrition is in our soul, our willpower. But we are not just souls, we are also flesh. We need to be mortified. Mortification is willingness to suffer. It is rooted in the body and controls the appetite, the pleasures.

How do we overcome our passion well? Pope Benedict XIV in a 1741 encyclical wrote, "With the fast, almost a mark of our militia, we are distinguished from the enemies of the Church, we turn away the lightning of divine vengeance, and, with the help of God, we are protected in the course of the days from the Princes of darkness."[65] He also mentioned in the same encyclical the custom of adhering to a single meal during the days of Lent. The "...mark of our militia...," is synonymous to our spiritual combat. We overcome our passions by doing violence to our flesh, "...the kingdom of God suffereth violence, and the violent bear it away."[66] We look to the ancient Catholics to overcome our passions by fasting and abstinence.

In the first 1,000 years, the Lenten abstinence included no meat, eggs, milk, butter, or cheese. The Eastern Churches still practice this abstinence today. Bread with salt and herbs and water were the common foods during the abstinence. Fasting meant no food until Vespers during Holy Week. But in the centuries following this, the Church grew more liberal. Vespers was said in the middle of the day and the meal was taken at mid-day. The collation, a light meal, was introduced at this time in addition to the main meal. Later, a second collation, breakfast, was introduced in the morning consisting of bread and coffee. The word literally means to "break the fast." Finally, today we only are required by Canon Law to fast on Ash Wednesday and Good Friday, two days

---

64 Rm. viii: 28.
65 Pope Benedict XIV, Non Ambigimus, Encyclical, 1741.
66 Mt. xi: 12.

during Lent when the ancient Christians observed forty days, to imitate Our Lord Jesus Christ in the desert. Also, we only have six days of abstinence required in Canon Law. Every Friday was a norm last century. Although few people know it, canon law still requires abstinence from meat every Friday, but outside of Lent, another penance may be substituted.

St. Thomas helps us to understand how to overcome our uncontrolled passions in our modern age. Abstinence is refraining from certain kinds of food and it is a virtue and a part of temperance.[67] Fasting is refraining eating from food in general. It too is a virtue and a part of temperance.[68]

St. Thomas goes on to explain according to St. Gregory the Great, why the forty days are observed. First, the Decalogue is accomplished in the four books of the Gospels, and ten times four is forty. Second, our bodies are made of four elements, and we should punish that body, which transgresses the Decalogue, forty times. Third, under the Law it was commanded that tithes should be paid of things, so we pay God a tithe of days, for since a year is composed of three hundred and sixty-five days, by punishing ourselves for thirty-six days, namely the fasting days during the six weeks of Lent, we pay God a tithe of our year.[69]

St. Thomas then goes on to explain that it is the custom of the Christian people to eat once a day, the faster's meal is eaten after 3:00 PM, and those who fast are bidden to abstain from flesh meat, eggs, and milk foods, as it too is the custom of the Church.[70]

What ever happened to SALT? Three of us made a pilgrimage to Rome which changed my life. I met some priests from the diocese of Wichita who were there at the time, Monsignor Conley and Father Coakley. They both inspired me, for the first time, with a great love of the Church and her holy customs. They both have moved on to become successors of the Apostles. Through the penances of SALT, nocturnal adoration, praying the Rosary publicly at the abortion clinic, and observing fasting as a group, I was introduced to the virtue of temperance, fortitude, mortification, fasting, and abstinence. These virtues are important

---

[67] ST, II-II, Q. 146, Art. 1.
[68] ST, II-II, Q. 147, Art. 1.
[69] ST, II-II, Q. 147, Art. 5.
[70] ST, II-II, Q. 147, Art. 6, 7, 8.

in spiritual combat and will help us to move away from the vices of gluttony, drunkenness, lust, fornication, and anger.

How does one practice the virtues of fasting and abstinence? First, pray a decade of the Rosary stating each virtue before each Our Father and Hail Mary for a time, perhaps a month. Also ask for the virtue of prudence. Then, with the help of a Confessor or someone who is sound in the spiritual life, ask for advice on how to move forward with fasting and abstinence. Prudence is required because it takes time, maybe even years, for our bodies to adjust to fasting, to build up to the virtues in the soul and in the body. Also, it is important to eat food that is nutritious, not processed food or food that lacks vitamins. Balance is also a key. So with the help of both a competent spiritual director or confessor and a health doctor, one will have the objective means to arrive at a fast and abstinence that is pleasing to God and good for the soul and body, and will help one to get on the road to heaven.

Chapter Ten

Problem RUDENESS
Solution AFFABILITY

Since our human family is plunging headlong into depression, sadness, and vice, people treat each other poorly. They don't return calls, letters, or even greetings of "hello." People are just rude to each other. As I walk the streets of St. Joseph, some curse and flip me off, and some even rev up their smog-making monster trucks, trying to suffocate me in their diesel soot. We have got to turn this culture around with the help of God.

The spiritual dynamos of the world are contemplative religious. I had the privilege to give a retreat to some religious sisters preparing for the investiture. Two young women were preparing with a weeklong retreat to become novices, or "new" religious. The ceremony included these two young women entering the Church in wedding gowns to show their betrothal to become Spouses to Jesus Christ. Later they received the implements of the holy habit: the veil, the cincture, the Rosary, the scapular, and the book of Psalms. I remember telling them in the retreat words of St. Scholastica, "If men knew the peace which religious enjoy in retirement, the entire world would become one great convent." One of the most difficult things to do is to live the common life as religious with men who are not part of a natural family. But the Apostles and believers at the beginning lived in community, "And the multitude of believers had but one heart and one soul: neither did anyone say that aught of the things which he possessed, was his own; but all things were common onto them."[71]

---

71 Act. vi: 32.

The religious, especially contemplative religious and semi-contemplative religious, live an intense life rooted in religion. The virtue of religion is defined as rendering to God His due, principally by atonement and adoration. Atonement is sacrifice and penance to make reparation for sins past and present and the sins of other sinners. Part of the sacrifice in religious life is living in common. Many saints and holy authors have written how to live in this unique way of life. Fraternal charity is what makes this life possible and even joyful. In short, fraternal charity is lived by putting our wishes and desires below everyone else and uniting our hearts to the particular sentiments the Sacred Heart of Jesus and the Immaculate Heart of Mary have for us. All the virtues are needed to live the life in common. Religious communities that have a great amount of virtue can teach the world by their example. "A new commandment I give unto you: that you love one another, as I have loved you, that you also love one another. By this shall all men know that you are my disciples, if you have love for one another."[72] One of these virtues is called friendliness.

Ever since the fall, our human family has developed enmity amongst each other. Cain killed Abel. The virtue of justice, giving to each other his due, helps us to restore relationships with each other. Friendliness is part of the virtue of justice.[73] St. Thomas calls it *affability* and classifies it as a virtue. Affability is acting in a becoming manner towards other men in mutual relations, with one another, and in words and deeds.[74]

What are some specific ways to be affable? In your speech, "...be yea, yea: no, no: and that which is over and above these is evil."[75] In other words, when people ask legitimate questions, affability requires a clear response. It is pitiful how so many people do not answer legitimate questions. Also, it is affable to make commitments with people when an invitation is given. It is an honor to be asked as a guest at a banquet, a wedding, or some event large or small. The host deserves a clear "yes" or "no." Once a commitment is made, one must keep in the virtue of affability, unless the change in commitment is required. For

---

72 Jn. xiii: 34 – 35.
73 ST. Pt. II-II, Q. 114, Art. 2.
74 ST. Pt. II-II, Q. 114, Art. 1.
75 Mt. v: 37.

example, if one commits to an invitation, but a better invitation arrives, it is a defect of affability to choose the better invitation, unless it is reasonable. For example, a poor woman invites you to a fast food restaurant. You commit to the meal but get an invitation from a noble family at the same time. It is against affability not to show up at the fast food restaurant, while the poor woman waits for you as you go to the noble table. She deserves you to fulfill your commitment or to ask her to reschedule.

The two defects of affability are flattery and quarreling. Flattery is defined as a man who wishes always to speak pleasantly to others, exceeding the mode of friendliness with the intention of making some gain out of it.[76] Quarreling consists of words, when, namely, one person contradicts another's words.[77] Generally speaking, quarreling is worse than flattery.

What would the world be like if we all strove to be affable? It would be a foretaste of heaven. There was a time called Christendom when one could stand on a hill in Europe and see various and sundry monasteries, convents, and abbeys dotting the tops. Saints filled these walls and they interceded on behalf of all peoples for the help of God to live with each other in charity. We need to have a time in our world today when many souls want to strive to become saints, where the culture makes taboo adultery, fornication, and other sins. The Church has all the answers to all the problems of the world. Say the Rosary for the virtue of affability. Receive Holy Communion for friendliness to enter your soul. Make fastings and long prayers to get along with each other, to practice for heaven.

---

76 ST. Pt. II-II, Q. 115, Art. 1.
77 ST. Pt. II-II, Q. 116, Art. 1.

Chapter Eleven

Problem A QUARRELSOME SPIRIT

Solution FRIENDSHIP

One sweltering hot day in spring, as I was studying Latin under a tree next to a bus stop by St. Joseph's city hall, a man sat next to me and began to discuss religion and psychology. After several minutes moving from his past in a mental ward, his sins of the flesh, and children he had that he did not know, he allowed me to talk about repenting for past sins and how to get out of mental sins with the truth.

"Our minds are made for the truth. When we speak lies, we damage our intellect because we make lies, and our minds are meant only for truth. This not only offends God, and is sinful, but brings about sickness and death. Our system does not accept a lie because we are made for the truth. Our bodily processes go awry when we lie."

In our conversation, he brought up the Bible allowing me to know that he does read it. I invited him, "How would you like to repeat a prayer with me? It comes from Luke Chapter 1. It is the 'Hail Mary' prayer." The prayer from the Rosary comes from Luke Chapter 1: 28, "Hail, full of grace, the Lord is with thee: blessed art thou among women." Luke Chapter 1: 42 has another part of the prayer, "...and blessed is the fruit of thy womb." After I explained this to him, I asked him, "Would you like to repeat it with me?" He said, "No."

At that moment, I knew that he was obstinate and had a quarreling spirit. I knew because of what I had experienced in our conversation, and he had a lack of devotion and honor toward the Mother of God, which is a sign that one is not predestined to heaven. "The learned and pious Jesuit, Suarez, the erudite and devout Justus Lipsius, doctor of Louvain, and many others have proved invincibly, from the sentiments of the Fathers (among others, St. Augustine, St. Ephrem, deacon of Edessa, St. Cyril of Jerusalem, St. Germanus of Constantinople, St. John Damascene, St. Anselm, St. Bernard, St. Bernardine, St. Thomas, and St. Bonaventure), that devotion to our Blessed Lady is necessary to salvation, and that it is an infallible mark of reprobation to have no esteem and love for the holy Virgin; while on the other hand, it is an infallible mark of predestination to be entirely and truly devoted to her."[78]

During our conversion I asked, "Do you think that you are going to heaven or hell?" He pointed down. I wanted to help him point up after our conversation. Immediately after, I was silent, and a bystander began to explain the eternal truths of salvation to him, trying to get him to change. But after about half an hour, he flared up, exhibiting his quarreling spirit by moving his arms up and down vigorously. He dramatically got up off the wall and walked away from both of us, sending us a message by his body language which I judged as, "He thinks he won the battle here. But he may lose the war for his soul."

St. Thomas says the quarreling spirit is opposed to friendship and affability. "Quarreling consists properly in words, when, namely, one person contradicts another's words."[79] St. Thomas goes on to explain this as a contradiction and gives two distinctions: 1) discord,[80] or 2) quarreling. Here quarreling is distinguished as when "...contradiction arises by reason of the speaker being a person to whom someone does not fear to be

---

[78] St. Louis de Montfort, True Devotion to Mary, Translated by Fr. Faber, Tan Books and Publishers, Inc., Rockford, Illinois, 1985, no. 40, p. 23.
[79] ST. Pt. II-II, Q. 116, Art. 1.
[80] St. Thomas says this discord is a lack of love for the person speaking which unites the minds and is contrary to charity.

disagreeable.[81] But this is against the cardinal virtue of justice, to give to each other his due. Mankind dwells with each other, and it is important to observe justice and more specifically, affability and friendliness with those whom we meet.

In my observation, a quarreling spirit causes harm to many souls. Quarreling can retard relationships with people, preventing them from advancing in their work, or even making a living. Quarreling prevents one from seeing the truth because the quarreler thinks he is always right. He despises anyone who might oppose him. It becomes impossible to talk with a quarreler because he seems to be the center of every conversation because he is not open to hearing other opinions or even the truth. These people sometimes are very prideful and have a sense of being a victim of circumstances when it is this quarreling spirit that gets them into bad situations. Many people that live in the streets and attend the soup kitchens have a quarreling spirit. I walk by the soup kitchens and the homeless are there quarreling with each other. So in a word, rich or poor, young or old, any soul is capable of this vice. So what is the remedy?

Pray the Rosary to become a devotee of the Blessed Virgin Mary. Protestantism has a certain quarreling spirit against the Mother of God. In my observation, the Protestants I meet are smart people, but some have taken the poison, the propaganda of the lies and blasphemies against the Immaculate Heart of Mary. What they do not see is that God, in His divine economy, His plan, chose to use the Blessed Virgin Mary to bring about the Victory of the Cross. St. Louis de Montfort predicted that a group of great saints in the latter times shall be distinguished for their devotion to the Blessed Lady, "With one hand they shall fight, overthrow and crush the heretics with their heresies, the schismatics with their schisms, the idolaters with their idolatries and the sinners with their impieties."[82] We must pray the Rosary to overcome the spirit of quarreling, for the Blessed Virgin Mary is the example of gentleness and humility. She did not quarrel with the Archangel

---

81 ST. Pt. II-II, Q. 116, Art. 1.
82 St. Louis de Montfort, True Devotion to Mary, Translated by Fr. Faber, Tan Books and Publishers, Inc., Rockford, Illinois, 1985, no. 48, p. 27.

Gabriel after the Angelic Greeting, but said, "Fiat," "...be it done."[83] We should say decades of the Rosary, inserting the virtues in each decade of "justice," "gentleness," and "humility" before each "Our Father," and "Hail Mary," so that we can truly root out any spirit of quarreling.

---

83 Lk. i:38.

Chapter Twelve

Problem NO PEACE FROM NOISE AND DISTRACTION

Solution PEACE THROUGH SILENCE, ATTENTION AND ADORATION

The world is becoming noisier and more distracting. Cell phones, computers, and video games are retarding the attention span. Machines continually intrude on our lives with their agitating noise. Ultimately the world is drawing people further away from silence, attention, and adoration of God. But God is not found in noise. "...the Lord is not in the wind, and after the wind and earthquake: the Lord is not in the earthquake. And after the earthquake a fire: the Lord is not in the fire, and after the fire a whistling of a gentle air. And when Elias heard it, he covered his face with his mantle..."[84] For the "whistling of a gentle air" was God.

In my observation, people in general are plugged into to their ear phones, motorcyclists have radios that can be heard from two blocks away, children greet me with a video game in their hand, ceasing to play the game to look at me for more than a second or two, families eat meals in front of the television, and some cannot drive a car without the radio on every second. Silence is rare, but God is found in silence, or "the whistling of a gentle air."

---

84 3 Kings xix: 11-13.

I do not know if it has been scientifically proven, but someone told me that a bowl of water placed in a forest and one placed next to rap music at full blast can be measured in a certain way indicating that the molecules of the water in the forest have measurements of peace while the water next to the blaring speakers has measurements of agitation. Whether this is true or not, we know in spirituality that a soul can find peace in silence.

St. Thomas writes a few articles on peace, attention, and adoration. He places peace under the virtue of charity. In making a distinction of peace between one man and another and peace within a man, he mentions the appetites in the latter that tend to diverse objects causes a clashing of the movement of the appetites.[85] What does this mean? If a man's heart is divided between the world and God, he will never have what he wants, and never having what he wants will not bring peace within. That is why St. Augustine wrote in his autobiography, "You have made us for yourself O Lord, and our hearts are restless until they rest in you."[86] In order to have peace within, we must have God alone as our one object and reject the evils of the world. This can be done by repentance of our sinful desires of evil and reforming our life to be alone with God. Why does this work? The theological virtue of charity has God as the object. When we offer ourselves to Him and are doing His will in our lives, He provides us with a share of His life in us. How do we get charity? We ask for the virtue of charity. I have learned that asking for the virtue of charity in the Rosary is very efficacious because the Mother of God, whom God has chosen, is a great means to arrive at a great amount of charity. Since peace is the result of charity, the more we become full of charity, the more peaceful we shall become. I see this all the time when people have a great confidence in God, nothing however evil or bad, bothers them.

Now how does one get peace in this noisy, distracting world? St. Thomas gives us some principles that help us arrive at peace. He puts prayer and adoration under the virtue of religion. So what is religion? Religion is giving God His due. What is God's due? God is due prayer and adoration. Prayer is an internal act of

---

85 ST. Pt. II-II, Q. 29, Art. 1.
86 St. Augustine, Confessions, Lib. 1, 1-2, 2.5, 5: CSEL 33 (1-5).

religion and adoration is an external act of religion. Is attention a necessary condition of prayer? St. Thomas says attention is absolutely necessary for prayer. The end of prayer is God and keeping attention to God is most necessary.[87] So in essence we must be internally recollected, quieted in order to give God attention in prayer.

Looking at the exterior acts of religion, St. Thomas writes, since we are composed of a twofold nature, intellectual and sensible, we offer God a twofold adoration; namely, a spiritual adoration, consisting of the internal devotion of the mind mentioned above; and a bodily adoration which consists in an exterior humbling of the body. Exterior adoration is offered on account of interior adoration, in other words we exhibit signs of humility in our bodies in order to incite our affections to submit to God, since it is connatural to us to proceed from the sensible to the intelligible.[88]

Kneeling, folding our hands, and in general having a sense of the sacred when we come to pray in our souls and in our bodies helps to bring a reverence in our relationship with God. External acts of reverence bring about humility in the soul, the key to happiness. Thus, silence, adoration, attention and peace will allow us to be very happy in this life.

---

[87] ST. Pt. II-II, Q. 83, Art. 13.
[88] ST. Pt. II-II, Q. 84, Art. 1.

Chapter Thirteen

Problem   THE BELIEF THAT TRUTH COMES FROM WITHIN

Solution   UNDERSTANDING TRUTH COMES FROM GOD

      As Brother Joseph and I were walking through a quaint neighborhood, several boys riding their bikes asked, "What are you?" I explained, "I am a Roman Catholic Priest, and I am sent by God to help you get to Heaven. I do not want anyone in town to go to hell, so I come out here walking and praying the Rosary for the conversion of sinners." After doing some street preaching, I said, "Now kneel down for the blessing from God." Five of the six boys knelt down for the blessing, and in my observation, looking upon their faces, they seemed to have mixed looks of bewilderment and excitement. Across the street, from the backyard of an elegant old-style house, came a woman in her sixties saying, "Father, I am not Catholic, but my husband takes me to church. As I was preparing dinner, I saw those boys receive your teaching and then I lost it and began to cry when I saw them kneel down for your blessing." I asked her why she had not converted to the Catholic Church. "Now this experience has brought you to tears, why don't you consider becoming Catholic? Our Lord Jesus Christ established only one Church. All the other "churches" were founded by mere men and not Jesus, who is truly divine!" All she could say was that she was never becoming Catholic. I challenged her, bringing home the point, "Who founded your 'church?'" All she could say was, "Yes," not answering any of my questions.

"...[A]nd the truth shall make you free."[89] This woman was so moved by an external expression of the mission given to us by the authority of Our Lord Jesus Christ, "...Go ye into the whole world, and preach the gospel to every creature,"[90] yet she did not give herself over to the conversion of heart that God was giving her through the fulfillment of this command of Jesus as his chosen, anointed, priest was imparting the blessing of the Holy Trinity on these boys. She was not freed from the slavery of the children of the lie. I do not know what was in her heart, but at that moment she did not manifest the conversion externally that this witness should have provided.

In my observation, there are certain very strong spirits that move people to think that the truth is within. This is such a covert and pernicious lie that so few souls are aware that it is a cancer to their soul and a danger to their eternal salvation. So many people say to me, "Father, my loved one is in Heaven. I just feel it," or "I feel that there are many paths to God, not just the Catholic Church," or "Father, I worship God from home. I do not need to go to Mass anymore." These wicked and strong spirits are deeply rooted in our human family. In my observation, the thirteenth century was the height of Christendom. It has been a downward spiral since then and has been accelerated in the last decades. There are many evil, nefarious spirits that are corporately moving our human family deeper into the lie. They are a revolutionary spirit against God. The three typical sources are the flesh, the world, and the devil. The chief of these revolutionary spirits is as St. Thomas notes, unbelief. Two species of unbelief are heresy and apostasy.

Unbelief is a sin "in which a man refuses to hear the faith, or despises it."[91] It is the greatest of sins.[92] Heresy is an assent to Christ, but choosing not what Christ really taught, but

---

89 Jn. xiii: 32.
90 Lk. xvi: 15.
91 ST II-II, Q. 10, Art. 1.
92 ST II-II, Q. 10, Art. 3.

the suggestion of his own mind.[93] Apostasy in general means to give up and withdraw from the faith all together.[94] The spirits of unbelief, heresy and apostasy are more or less the result of people who think the truth comes from within. In our spiritual combat, I observe on the streets how people make that fatal error believing that truth comes from within them. But this is wrong because man is prone to make errors, and when we rely on ourselves for the truth apart from God, we will eventually err. This error, when it grows to maturity, generally causes unbelief, heresy and apostasy. Our generation is saturated with this way of thinking, and it makes it extremely difficult to reason with people who chose to stay in this error.

What is the remedy for people who think in these ways? Truth is the good of the intellect. Since the intellect is designed and ordered toward knowing the truth, when it knows the truth, there is a completion or perfection of its nature. Since truth is the rectitude of the intellect, then falsity is the deformation of the intellect. As truth is the conformity of the intellect to reality, truth puts us in contact with reality. We must learn to conform ourselves to reality and not expect reality to conform itself to us.[95]

Once people realize this error and have the humility to conform themselves to reality, it will be easier for them to conform themselves to God.

For example, the lady who was mentioned at the beginning of the chapter can easily allow that experience of seeing those boys kneel for the blessing of God to cause her to conform herself to reality, the reality that God sent his Son, Our Lord Jesus Christ, to establish One Church for the way of her salvation. I pray that I see her again, so that God will continue to sweetly and gently move her to conform herself to reality. Maybe there was some scandal that was real or perceived, that a member of the Catholic Church may have done, that prevents her from looking into the Church. Whatever the reason may be, it is important for us to conform ourselves to reality. Our Lord Jesus Christ said, "The truth will set you free." How do we do this?

93 ST II-II, Q. 11, Art. 1.
94 ST II-II, Q. 12, Art. 1.
95 Fr. Ripperger, Chad, Ph. D., Introduction to the Science of Mental Health, Vol. 1: Philosophical Psychology, 2001, Chad Ripperger, p. 311-313.

Pray the Rosary sincerely and devoutly for the virtue of humility. When we repeat some of the words from St. Luke's Gospel, we are driving the spirits of unbelief, heresy and apostasy away from us, so we have a chance to be changed by the truth which is reality and God. We should also join a Confraternity of the Holy Face of Jesus to pray for the conversion of sinners. Jesus revealed to Sr. Mary of St. Peter on November 22, 1846 in the Carmel of Tours, "By My Holy Face you will obtain the conversion of many sinners. Nothing that you ask in making this offering will be refused to you. If you knew how pleasing the sight of My Face is to My Father!"

Chapter Fourteen

Problem FORGETTING ABOUT JUDGEMENT DAY

Solution REMEMBERING THE FOUR LAST THINGS

The majority of people who walk up to me in the streets tell me as Patricia said, "Father, there are many paths to heaven – Christianity, Buddhism, Pagan worship." Or Robert, "I know in my heart that my mom is done suffering because she is in a better place." Unfortunately, I must correct their thinking and preach the Four Last Things: Death, Judgment, Heaven, and Hell. If we believe in these four things, it makes it easier for us to stop committing sin. It is good to keep our death in mind, not in an unbalanced morbid way, but in a healthy way. Once our body and soul separate, our destiny to either Hell or Heaven is sealed for eternity. It is a good thing to think of our particular judgment and our General Judgment. When we die, each of us will see Our Lord Jesus Christ, and He will reward the good and punish the bad. Think of the moment before He declares our place in eternity... Heaven or Hell. After that, we receive our reward or punishment, Heaven[96] or Hell. Then at the end of time is the General Judgment.

Who will judge and who will be judged at the General Judgment? It is a common belief by Christians, Jews, and Muslims that the Valley of Josaphat[97] is where the General Judgment will take place. The General Judgment will make public all the decrees of Our Lord Jesus Christ.

---

96 Some to Purgatory then to Heaven.
97 Joel iii: 2, 12.

St. Thomas asks who will judge and who will be judged.[98] Then he asks whether any men will judge together with Christ. The answer is yes, the perfect will acquaint others of the sentence delivered on the authority of Our Lord Jesus Christ. So it belongs to the elect to repeat the codex of the law.[99]

And this makes sense when the just are persecuted by sinners. We hope not for the death of sinners but for their conversion.[100] But if that does not happen in their lifetime, they are punished for the evil they did. Those that follow Christ in giving everything away for His sake are the ones who will judge with Christ unrepentant sinners at the General Judgment. Jesus said, "...you, who have followed[101] me in the regeneration, when the Son of man shall sit on the seat of His majesty you also shall sit on the twelve seats judging the twelve tribes of Israel."[102] St. Thomas comments that poverty corresponds to judicial power.[103] He also observes that sinners have subjected themselves to the devil by sinning; therefore, it is just that they are subjected and accused to the devils.[104] All judicial power has been given by the Father to Our Lord Jesus Christ by the humility showed in His Passion.[105]

So after reading this, the hope is, when meeting people who opine about universal salvation, we can bear a couple of things in our minds. First, justice is a virtue where each is truly given his due. Second, if we are persecuted for doing good, it is important to allow God to take vengeance, not ourselves. The temptation is to take vengeance into our own hands. Sometimes it is prudent to exact justice, but sometimes it is prudent to let the will of God be made manifest. If we truly serve God in this life, the hope is that our persecutors will change and do good by the charity of our action, but if that does not happen, and we have left everything to follow Christ, we will someday have our reward. St. Peter asked, "Behold we have left all things and have followed Thee: what therefore shall we have?"[106] Jesus answers St. Peter

---

98 ST III, Q. 89.
99 ST III, Q. 89, A. 1.
100 Ez. xviii: 23.
101 "Left all things" in the Summa
102 Mt. xix: 28.
103 ST III, Q. 89, A. 2.
104 ST III, Q. 89, A. 4.
105 ST III, Q. 89, A. 5.
106 Mt. xix, 27.

with the verse above, telling him that he will judge the twelve tribes of Israel, in other words those who persecuted him and martyred him who died unrepentant.

So what does this teach us when we meet people who speak of everyone going to heaven, or so-and-so is in a better place? With all gentleness, we do well to correct their thinking at the right time. Fraternal charity means we want to remove people from their error. We wish for them to come to heaven by removing the obstacle of error.

How can this be done? First, give them a Rosary and a Miraculous Medal. Teach them to pray it especially contemplating the Fifth Sorrowful Mystery, the Crucifixion and the Death of Our Lord Jesus Christ. When we are the object of scorn, we should recite the prayer, "O Mary conceived without sin, pray for us," keeping in mind, the conversion of the sinner and not his death is the desire of God.

We can ask questions. Does God force people to live in heaven? Since evil is not in heaven, how can someone who wishes only evil, without desiring to change, live in heaven?

Knowledge of the truth helps us to be good because the truth sets us free, free from the lie. So the hope is that when being persecuted for Christ's sake, we can know the reality of the situation and endure it with patience.

Chapter Fifteen

Problem THINKING WE ARE PERFECT
Solution UNDERSTANDING GOD IS PERFECT

"Be you therefore perfect, as also your heavenly Father is perfect" (Mt. 5: 48).

As a young man and I were walking around Baltimore, Maryland, a middle-aged man approached us and said, "My ways are perfect." I thought, "This ought to be quite an interesting dialogue." He went on to explain to us that his private religion was better and "more perfect" than our Catholic Religion. After explaining to him that God gave us the Catholic Church through Jesus, the great Redeemer, and the Church has the answer for every problem, he went ballistic and said, "My ways are perfect. Your ways are in error!" I said, "Okay, if your ways are perfect, are you perfect?" After he said yes, I asked, "What is three to the third power?" The story continues below.

How does the Catholic Church explain growing in perfection since Our Lord Jesus Christ commands us to be perfect as his Father is in heaven? Fr. Reginald Garrigou-Lagrange, O.P. wrote a number of books on perfection in the spiritual life. I take much from his summary book on perfection *The Three Conversions in the Spiritual Life*.[107]

---

107 Garrigou-Lagrange, O. P., The Three Conversions in the Spiritual Life, Tan Books and Publishers, Rockford, Illinois, 2002. Original copyright year: 1938.

There are three levels in the spiritual life that tend toward perfection: the purgative way, the illuminative way, and the unitive way. They are also synonymous to beginner, proficient and perfect. "...[T]he development of the interior life has often been compared to the three periods or stages of the physical life, childhood, youth, and manhood." St. Thomas himself has indicated this analogy.[108]

The purgative way is the soul trying to overcome mortal sin. This was St. Peter when he was called by Jesus to follow him. The illuminative way is the soul no longer struggling to overcome mortal sin but trying to purify its motives since it is in the service of the Lord. One in the illuminative way has what is called a mercenary love because one is in the state of grace but serves God for a temporal or spiritual reason. This is St. Peter when he denied Jesus three times. St. Thomas says that after St. Peter mortally sinned by denying Jesus three times, his contrition was so strong that it brought him back to the state of grace, but also most likely elevated him to a higher state of perfection.[109] Our Lord allowed this fall to help St. Peter see that he is nothing without the Lord. The unitive way is the soul who serves God for his sake and without fear. This was St. Peter when he received the Holy Ghost at Pentecost. He was happy to suffer persecution when professing boldly about the Savior. He was jailed twice and given stripes. Three thousand converted in one day. The Acts of the Apostles are full of these men who are in the unitive way, St. Stephen being one of the first. They had a certain sense of contemplation of God, and He gave them an illumination and a strength to start the Church and proclaim the kingdom of God.

When one compares the three states of spiritual perfection to physical life, it is easy to see how important it is to move forward on the road of perfection. Childhood lasts to puberty around age fourteen, adolescence lasts from about age fourteen to twenty, and then manhood from twenty to about thirty-five, which is considered full manhood.[110]

It is easy to see how a young boy must grow into a young man physically and mentally or he will assume some positive bias

---

108 Ibid., p. 25 - 26.
109 ST, III, Q. lxxxix., art. 2. "Wherefore the penitent sometimes arises to a great grace than that which he had before." 'Contingit intensionem motus poenitentis quandoque proportionatume esse majori gratiae.'
110 Ibid., p. 26.

toward evil, or remain a half-wit, perhaps a complete idiot, for the rest of his life.

"It is at this point that the analogy becomes illuminating for the spiritual life. We shall see that the beginner who fails to become a proficient, either turns to sin or else presents an example of arrested spiritual development. Here too, it is true that 'he who makes no progress loses ground,' as the Fathers of the Church have so often pointed out."[111]

There are three conversions in the interior life. The first is to the purgative way, the second to the illuminative and the third to the unitive way. All three are painful, but the last two are not only awful, but confusing. That is why so few people even enter the interior life. They are always in the state of mortal sin or at best in and out of it. The reason the last two are so painful is that most souls think they are doing something wrong, because God withdraws his consolations. This is where a good Confessor or spiritual director can guide the soul through these difficult times.

The interesting thing is that everyone is called by God to the unitive state, the state of perfection as Our Lord commands. But there are so few people who engage in the interior life. In order to get to heaven, one needs to die in the state of grace, with no mortal sin on the soul. Going through these conversions will help to make this happen. Not only that, the higher one gets in the life of perfection, the greater will be his glory in heaven.

How does one begin? Read the Garrigou-Lagrange book mentioned above, *The Three Conversions in the Spiritual Life*. Ask an experienced priest to help you get through the second and third conversion. Pray the Rosary for union with God. Desire a life void of mortal sin. Go to Confession on a regular basis. Carve out in your day some time for spiritual reading. Attend Mass daily if possible.

So what happened to the "perfect" man in Baltimore? After asking him, "What is three to the third power?" He answered, "Nine." I said, "Nope, it is 27 (3 x 3 x 3)." He said, "Well, I was not very good at math, but I am still perfect." I said, "No, the definition of perfect is one who does not make an error." To which he answered, "My ways are perfect and yours are not." There comes a time when a soul like his just rejects the known truth.

---

111 Ibid., p. 27.

This does great damage to the intellect which seeks the truth. Some people just live the lie, but I do pray that this man will come to realize that the truth will set him free. That is why I walk the streets to find souls who are searching for the truth.

St. Peter did the same, and eventually his love for Jesus Christ caused him to be crucified upside down in the Eternal City, Rome.

Chapter Sixteen

Problem THE GOAL OF JUST BARELY
MAKING IT TO HEAVEN

Solution UNDERSTANDING THE REWARDS
OF HEAVEN

As I was walking around St. Joseph, Missouri one day, a young woman came to me and asked, "Why do you go walking around?" I answered, "To save souls from Hell and to teach good souls to be better." To which she answered, "All I want is to just barely get into heaven." The story will continue below after a study on the degrees of glory in heaven.

"In my Father's house are many mansions."[112] The word *mansion* is called "establishment," or in Latin *collocatio,* setting up, erecting, placing. St. Thomas speaks about things moving, and once arriving, they stop and rest. The end of the movement is a place or a mansion, or a place of rest or an end to a journey.[113] The thought is that each person who enters heaven will have a mansion in which to rest for eternity. We can observe in a city that there are mansions of various sizes. We can even describe a dwelling in a hierarchical way, cardboard house, shack, barn, apartment, duplex, family home, ranch, mansion, castle and palace.

---
112 St. John xiv: 2.
113 ST, Suppl. Q 93, Art. 2.

In eschatology, the branch of theology that is concerned with the ultimate or last things such as death,[114] we observe that there are different levels of glory in heaven. How does one end up in a large mansion? First, we know that in death the soul and the body separate. St. Cyril in one of his epistles to St. Augustine relates what was told to him by a man who was raised from the dead. "The moment when my soul left its body, was one of such awful pain and distress that none can imagine the anguish I then endured. If all conceivable suffering and pain were put together they would be as nothing compared with the torture I underwent at the separation of the soul and body."[115] Then we know after death there is the judgment, particular and general, and "...it is appointed unto men once we die, and after this the judgment..."[116] After the general judgment, each soul will go to eternal reward in heaven or eternal punishment in hell. "Come, ye blessed of my Father possess you the kingdom prepared for you from the foundation of the world,"[117] and "...depart from me, you cursed, into everlasting fire...".[118] Those that go to heaven will follow St. Michael, who will take the true cross relic, and each will go according to rank, infants and deathbed conversion, God-fearing married people, priests, saintly bishops, doctors of the church, confessors, martyrs, holy virgins, and the holy apostles led by each choir respective of rank.[119]

And then each will go to his mansion according to his charity. St. Thomas says the more one will be united to God, the happier one will be. This is measured by charity, and the diversity of charity will be the diversity of beatitude or glory.[120]

So how is charity measured? Our actions are meritorious, not so much by the substance of the action, but by the purity of

---

114 "Eschatology" The American Heritage Dictionary, 1991.

115 Fr. Von Cochem, Martin, O.S.F.C., The Four Last Things: Death, Judgment, Hell, Heaven, Tan Books and Publishers, Rockford, Illinois, 1987, p. 9.

116 Hebrews ix: 27.

117 Mt. xxv: 34.

118 Mr. xxv: 41.

119 Fr. Von Cochem, Martin, O.S.F.C., The Four Last Things: Death, Judgment, Hell, Heaven, Tan Books and Publishers, Rockford, Illinois, 1987, p. 110-112.

120 ST, Suppl. Q. 93, Art. 3.

intention or habit of virtue in which they are done. For example, a hermit who was very holy by his fervent love of God, who saved no soul directly because he met no one in his solitude, will have a higher place in heaven than a missionary who was used as an instrument of God to save 100,000 souls but he did it out of vainglory. Assuming that both go to heaven, the hermit will have a mansion that is greater in the Divine vision than the missionary. Lastly, since charity should be sought after by itself, the diversity of merit will distinguish the mansions by way of merit.[121] So we do well to build up the kingdom of God by Him moving us to do good works, like feeding the hungry, clothing the naked, housing the homeless, instructing the ignorant, correcting the faults of our neighbor, and encouraging the weak. But the most important thing is to love God, because He loved us first. We need to study the Great Commandment to love God above all things, to meditate on the value of His Precious Blood and to have a desire to save souls who are in great peril.

For those who desire to receive a great mansion, they must first know that it is by God alone that we will get there. All the good that we ever do comes from God; we cannot do anything to get to heaven on our own. It is through the merit of Jesus Christ that we are saved. The great act of charity is to go to Calvary several times a day. One may ask, how can I go there several times a day if I do not live there? The answer is to go to the Most Holy Sacrifice of the Mass. The *Pieta* prayer book has a section titled *Graces Derived from Assisting at Mass*. There are sixteen points worth reading. My favorite is number thirteen, *Every Mass wins for you a higher degree of glory in Heaven!*[122] So try to go to Mass as often as you can with the right disposition, charity. Try to go several times a week, or every day, or even twice or three times a day. My old spiritual director, Fr. Walter Karrer, C.Ss.R., would say Mass at 8:00 AM, and then I would see him at the noon Mass at the Cathedral in Wichita, Kansas. I asked him, "Father, why do you go to all these Masses?" To which he smiled, "I also go to the 5:30 PM at Our Lady of Perpetual Help, if I am able. The reason I go there is because the priest is Jesus. When Jesus

---
121 Ibid.
122 Pieta, p. 26.

elevates the Holy Eucharist and the Precious Blood, those are the most privileged times to petition God." Since then, I love being able to say Mass and then attend in choir in cassock and surplice so I can really concentrate and meditate on my petitions to Jesus, who is there.

Dear reader, maybe you are not able to go to multiple Masses a day. If not now, start making steps to make it happen soon! For if you attend Masses with charity, your glory will be increased one degree for each Mass you attend.

So to continue our story, after a little more conversation, I told her, "When I go to the judgment seat of Jesus, I hope to tell Him, 'You see these 150,000 souls that I met in the streets, I tried to tell them about You.' Then I hope that Jesus will be merciful to me at my judgment. I hope on that terrible day of my judgment, that he will say, 'Come and enter into your inheritance prepared from the beginning of time.' We should not try to just barely make it to heaven, but do all in our strength to love God above all things, to love his Most Sacred Host, His Most Precious Blood, and desire to save souls by bringing them to the Holy Sacrifice of the Mass."

Chapter Seventeen

Problem — THE NOTION THAT EVERYONE IS GOING TO HEAVEN

Solution — HOPE. THE NECESSARY VIRTUE TO GET TO HEAVEN

Walking the streets one day, someone came up to me, "Why do you wear black?" To which I responded, "It is to remind us that we die to ourselves and obey another. I have placed myself under the obedience of a bishop. Black reminds me of that." She said, "Oh, I have many friends and family who have died. They are all in a better place."

This lady is not the only person whom I have heard saying that "everyone is going to heaven." I often hear it at funerals, "Mom is in a better place." But we have to be careful about this line of thinking. If everyone is going to heaven, then why do we need a Redeemer and His Church? St. Thomas breaks down the correct way of thinking about the virtue of hope.

The Angelic Doctor states that presumption is a man who, "...despises the Divine Justice, which punishes the sinner."[123] Presumption is an inordinate conversion to God, an immoderate hope in relying on his own power and not on God. Now God gives us the Ten Commandments to follow in order to be in friendship

---
123 ST, Pt. II-II, Q. 21, A. 1.

with him. But if a man continues to break the Commandments and not wish to reconcile with God, he is not a friend of God and cannot go to heaven if he dies in the state of mortal sin. For example, if one commits adultery during his life without reconciling to God but expects to die in that state without repentance and live forever in heaven, he is also committing the sin of presumption. He is missing the mark by an immoderate hope in God.

Hope is a future good, difficult but possible to obtain by ourselves or by others. Hope of eternal life is only possible by God on whose help it leans.[124] Hope is one of the theological virtues. By theological virtues the end is God Himself. Charity makes us adhere to God for His own sake. Faith makes us adhere to God by knowledge and truth. And hope makes us adhere to God by perfect goodness.

Concerning the theological virtues, those who already dwell with God no longer have faith, because object of faith is knowledge and truth of God without seeing Him, but the vision of Him removes faith, it is no longer necessary. Also, they no longer have hope, for the object of hope is a perfect future goodness, but since they have perfect goodness, hope is removed. But charity remains, for the object of charity is God Himself, and since they dwell with God, they have obtained a resting place in charity. We as wayfarers who obey God have a certainty of obtaining perfect goodness if we persevere in this way unto death.[125] "And now there remain faith, hope, and charity, these three: but the greatest of these is charity."[126]

Now what is the most important thing to do in life? It is to get to heaven. Our human family has disrupted our relationship with God first by our primary parents, Adam and Eve, and now by each of our actual sins. When these sins are serious enough, i.e. mortal, from the Latin word, "mors," "death," we have lost friendship with God. Salvation history is a continual story of spiritual death and reconciliation of Israel to God in the Old Covenant and the Holy Catholic Church to the Redeemer in the New Covenant of the Redeemer. Some individuals are constantly in and out of friendship with God by mortal sin and reconciliation.

---
124 ST, Pt. II-II Q. 17, A. 1.
125 ST, Pt. II-II, Q. 17, A. 6; Q. 18, A. 2 & 3.
126 I Cor. xiii: 13.

It is imperative to stay in friendship with God until death. God is giving us all the help to accomplish this even though He owes us nothing. Jesus Christ gave us seven signs to show that we are in friendship with Him. These signs are called "sacraments." In Latin, *sacra* means "holy." And *sacrament* means "sacred oath." These sacred oaths given to us by God through Jesus Christ, through the Blessed Virgin Mary, and finally through the Church instituted by Jesus Christ, are sacred oaths that make us holy, set apart for God. Of course, the soul receiving them must do so with all innocence. A sacrament does not give grace if the receiver is not authentic in his desire to be out of the state of mortal sin.

      The devil is always watching to devour us and take us from the friendship of God and ultimately to put us under his thumb in his kingdom, hell. St. Peter warns us, "Be sober and watch: because your adversary the devil, as a roaring lion, goeth about seeking whom he may devour. Whom resist ye, strong in faith: knowing that the same affliction befalls your brethren who are in the world."[127] So we have the perennial battle between heaven and hell that wages in every soul. This is the most difficult battle, but those who have hope obtain victory over the devil and live with God for eternity. Hope is our great spiritual weapon in attaining the perfect good. Hope is having a keen awareness of this battle and the rewards and punishments after this life. Our Lord Jesus Christ said, "Enter ye in at the narrow gate: for wide is the gate, and broad is the way that leadeth to destruction, and many there are who go in thereat."[128] These are words of mercy because Our Lord wishes us to work out our salvation now before it is too late. He gave us the Church to save us though the waters of Baptism. He gave us the Church to strengthen us through the sacred oath of Confirmation. He gave us the Church to give us spiritual food for our journey, as wayfarers, in the sacrament of Holy Communion. He gave us the Church to reconcile us through the sacrament of Penance. He gave us the Church to elevate love between a man and a woman as a sacred bond in which each partner helps the other get to heaven. He gave us the Church to build bridges,

---

127 I Peter v: 8-9.
128 St. Matt. vii:14.

whereby men in Holy Orders like deacons, priests, and bishops ("pontifex," or "bridge builder,") are mediators between mankind and God. They lay down their lives so the sheep can walk on their back like bridges from the nave "boat" of the church to the altar of God, or the gate of heaven. And lastly, He gave us the Church to encourage the sick in their last illnesses to go on the arduous journey of death, giving the soul spiritual unction to endure the journey with peace.

That is why it is ever more important now that during death and funerals we stop making God what He is not. "What good God would let people go to hell?" This is heresy. This is an error. This is leading many people to hell. Yes, it is true that God is good, he lets people go to hell, He has both perfect truth and charity and He leads us on the most sure and quickest path to Him. He gives us the way to Him through His Commandments and through His Church and through His Divine Son, Jesus. While walking the road to God we must be docile to Him as the Blessed Virgin Mary was docile. Her docility was so great the Holy Ghost flew to her and overshadowed her to produce the greatest thing ever, a God-Man. We should never speak out loud of our false opinion of God, but refer to what He has said about Himself, through his Scriptures, Sacred Tradition, and the Magisterium. That is the teaching of the Church held over the two millennia. When we too are docile, we will receive the gift of hope in God.

So to answer that lady I met, it is important to teach with all prudence those in error. Not everyone that says, "Lord, Lord, shall enter into the kingdom of heaven, but he that doeth the will of My Father who is in heaven, he shall enter into the kingdom of heaven." It is easy to get to heaven, but we have to try! We must follow the teachings of Jesus Christ and not just come up with our own Gospel. Our hope is in God who made heaven and earth.

Chapter Eighteen

Problem BELIEVING THAT THE ONLY HEAVEN IS HERE IN EARTH

Solution RECOGNIZING THAT LIFE ON EARTH IS FULL OF SUFFERING BUT IN HEAVEN THERE IS ONLY JOY

Unfortunately, many of the poor people I meet in the streets are drunk most of the time or are high on drugs. One day one of them came up to me slurring, "Preacher, there is no heaven, this is heaven!" To which I responded, "In heaven there is no suffering, but there are all kinds of sufferings here." This incident is to be continued below.

In the supplement to the *Summa Theologica*, St. Thomas lists four qualities of the resurrected: impassibility, subtlety, agility, and clarity. Impassibility is the freedom from suffering and corruption. "It is a common teaching of theologians that Adam and Eve had this condition before the Fall, but it has not been defined by the Church."[129]

A question in the *Summa* was asked, whether the bodies of the saints will be impassible after the resurrection. St. Thomas answers that a glorified body will not be subject to any suffering, so they are impassible.[130] Impassible bodies will be able to feel

---
129 A Catholic Dictionary, Donald Attwater, Tan Books and Publishers, Rockford, Illinois, 1997, 'Impassibility.'
130 ST, Q. 82, Art. 1.

sensations, but only pleasure. "The power of receiving pleasure through our senses is only a drop in the ocean when compared to our manifold capacities for suffering..."[131] in this world. But impassible resurrected bodies, "...will use their senses for pleasure insofar as this is not incompatible with the state of incorruption."[132] So there will be no more disease, headaches, broken bones, colds, flu, or scrapes. "And God shall wipe away all tears from their eyes; and death shall be no more, nor mourning, nor crying, nor sorrow shall be any more, for the former things are passed away."[133]

Everyone wants to be happy. Pleasure is feeling a great happiness. Everyone knows either consciously or subconsciously that we were made for happiness and pleasure, and there is something awfully wrong with suffering. The challenge is to know and believe what is to come after this world, specifically eternal pleasure or eternal pain. I often tell people to think of something pleasurable, walking barefoot on a sandy beach, receiving the rays of sun on your skin after a long and dark winter, or drinking that cup of coffee. Now take any pleasure that comes to mind and multiply it by a large number, ten, one hundred, one thousand, infinity. This gives us a better idea of the pleasures meant for those who enter into the kingdom of heaven.

The challenge is that we must die in the state of grace, i.e. no mortal sin on our soul. We are wise to give up forbidden pleasures of this world for they are passing, will not last forever, and can bring us to hell, where there is everlasting pain and suffering. So it is worth it to take faith seriously and commit no sin now to receive the reward of an impassable resurrected body, where there is only eternal pleasure and joy.

So back to the story. I continued, "It makes sense because of all the pain in the world to want to feel good for a while with drugs and alcohol, but it is a trap. Drugs damage our body and soul, and alcohol, if abused, damages our body and soul. But our human family has fallen from the state of preternatural grace enjoyed by Adam and Eve before they disobeyed the command of

---

131 Fr. J. Boudreau, S.J., *On the Happiness of Heaven: The Joys and Rewards of Eternal Glory*, Tan Publishers, Rockford, Illinois, 1984, p. 85.
132 Summa Contra Gentiles, Lib. 4, c. 86.
133 Apoc. xxi. 4.

God and took the forbidden fruit. They were cast out of the garden and were told that they would toil in work and bearing children. So we need to give thanks to God that he did not abandon us forever, for Jesus Christ has redeemed us from this state, but our redemption depends on our cooperation. We must serve Him as our King and die for him in the state of grace." I am not sure if this instruction changed his life, but I told him about Jesus Christ. And I am sure that Jesus Christ will do all that He can to win the soul back to Him. We do well, as Our Lady of Fatima told us, to pray for the conversion of sinners, including ourselves.

Chapter Nineteen

Problem LOSS OF THE BELIEF IN PURGATORY

Solution THE CHURCH'S MERCIFUL TEACHING OF PURGATORY

I was in a coffee shop when an older Catholic woman began talking to me. "As a nurse, I have seen the face of terror on only one person, after I coded him dead. Everyone else has gone to the light." Commenting on "everyone going to light (heaven)," I said, "There is also a place called Purgatory." To which she remarked, "I do not think so."

First, we need to remember that truth does not always come from within. We are human and prone to error. Immanentism is the idea that all truth comes from within. Since God is perfect and has revealed Himself to us, He has absolute truth. He has revealed Himself to us primarily in our times by His Visible Church instituted by the true Messiah Jesus of Nazareth.

The Church has given us the books that make up the Bible. The Old Testament has a proof of Purgatory. "It is therefore a holy and wholesome thought to pray for the dead, that they may be loosed from sins."[134] The Bible is without error and is interpreted by the Church. In the Catechism of the Council of Trent, it reads that Purgatory has fire, is founded in many holy Church councils,

---

134 II Macabees xii: 46.

confirmed by Apostolic tradition, and demands exposition from the pastor.[135] The Council of Trent in its Decree on Purgatory states that "there is a purgatory, and that the souls detained there are helped by the prayers of the faithful, especially by the acceptable Sacrifice of the Altar."[136]

Heathens and Jews even believe in a middle state. We find expiatory sacrifices for the dead among Africans, Chinese, Japanese, the Celts, Slavs, Greenlanders, North American Indian tribes, etc.[137]

As early as the second century, Tertullian wrote, "On the anniversaries of the dead we offer the Holy Sacrifice for the departed. Even though Scripture did not warrant this, the custom originates from tradition; it was confirmed by universal adoption and sanctioned by faith."

The suffering souls spend the amount of time that God has determined based on their venial sins and punishments due to their sins that were not satisfied during their time on earth. But in God's mercy, their time can be shortened.

St. Thomas speaks of the fires of purgatory as the same as hell. First, he states that a soul, having a venial sin that needs to be cleansed, goes to Hell, until it can resume its flight.[138] This is also what we call Purgatory. There is a fire in Hell and Purgatory that "...is really hurtful to the spirit...and the spirit is thus tormented by it."[139] Also, the same fire punishes the damned in hell and the just in Purgatory, and the least pain in Purgatory exceeds the greatest we can suffer in this world.[140]

It is important to know the consolation and not just the horror of Purgatory. St. Francis de Sales states, "Most persons

---

135 The Roman Catechism of the Council of Trent, Charlotte, North Caroline, Tan Books, p. 65.

136 The Church Teaches: Documents of the Church in English Translation, Jesuit Father of St. Mary's College, St. Mary's, Kansas, Tan Books Publishers, Rockford, Illinois, 1973, p. 352.

137 Nageleisen, Rev. John A., Charity for the Suffering Souls: An explanation of the Catholic Doctrine of Purgatory, Tan Books Publishers, Rockford, Illinois, 1982, p. 15.

138 ST III, Q. 69, A. 2.

139 ST III, Q. 70, A. 3.

140 Charity for the Suffering Souls, p. 49.

are afraid of Purgatory, because they regard themselves rather than the glory of God." He continues, "Great as the torments of Purgatory are, so that they cannot in any way be compared with the sufferings in this world, the interior consolations granted there are nevertheless so ineffable that no earthly bliss or enjoyment can equal them."[141]

With the evidence that Purgatory exists and the fire hurts, it is important to use this knowledge for practice. I hear people say that their loved ones are in a better place all too often. If they are really in Purgatory, this way of thinking is an offense to them. If you saw someone burning in a fire and could get them out with a rope or a stick, would you not do so? We would not just look at them and walk away. Ecclesiastical writers also note that superiors and priests often have to undergo a long and painful purgatory. This is because some people have such a high esteem for their office. That is why it is an important practice in some dioceses to ask all the priests to say three Masses for a priest after he dies.

The means of relieving the suffering souls are called suffrages. These include alms-deeds, fasting, and pilgrimages. But the best suffrage is to have Masses offered for them. Why is this the greatest? St. Alphonsus Liguori explains it well. "It was not necessary for the Redeemer to die in order to save the world; a drop of his blood, a single tear, or prayer was sufficient...But to institute the priesthood, the death of Jesus has been necessary."[142] How is this possible? At the Holy Sacrifice of the Mass, the priest *in persona Christi*[143] offers the holocaust to the Father in heaven. The offering of the death of Jesus, who is God, to His father, is a perfect offering. Not a better sacrifice could be given. This is applied to the soul in Purgatory as a suffrage, and in God's wisdom is used to lessen the time he has in Purgatory.

The funeral Mass of *Requiem*[144] makes this understandable in a visible sense. Vestments are black with a lining of gold, silver, or white. Black is a color that indicates death to show the fact that one has died. The lining of gold, silver, and especially white show

---

141 Charity for the Suffering Souls, p. 54.
142 St. Alphonsus de Liguori, Dignity and Duties of the Priest, Redemptorist Fathers, St. Louis, 1927, p. 26.
143 "In the person of Christ"
144 "Rest" from RIP, rest in peace

that when a soul departs to Purgatory, it is released by suffrages and puts on the white robe.[145] Pope Pius XII emphasized the importance not to take black vestments out of the arrangement that has been handed down from antiquity.[146]

One of the most memorable times in my life was when I offered the Requiem Mass for my departed Grandmother, Mary Covelli. I asked two of my priest friends to fill the role of Deacon and Sub-Deacon. The minor ministers were well trained. We were at historic St. Anthony's in Wichita, Kansas. The choir was wonderful, and the incense was full. The most special moment occurred when I was on the predella[147] offering to the Father His Son Jesus Christ on behalf of my grandmother, whose remains were in the coffin covered in a black pall. I thought to myself, "Grandma, this is the best thing I can do for you, your grandson a priest offering this perfect holocaust for you." After Mass, people were in tears saying things like, "I have not seen anything so beautiful in my life," "I have not seen a Requiem Mass in decades."

What ever happened to the nurse I met at the coffee shop? I invited her to come to Mass at the Abbey of Ephesus to hear the High Mass. I hope to see her. Death is difficult for us. It is not natural. It is easy to fall back on sophisms such as, "She is in a better place," etc. But the best expression and the most real is to live our lives knowing that it could end in either heaven or hell, with Purgatory as a time to delay the flight into heaven. The Requiem Mass is so balanced and beautiful. It is the best thing we can do for the dead. "It is therefore a holy and wholesome thought to pray for the dead, that they may be loosed from sins."[148]

---

145 Apoc. vi, 11.
146 Mediator Dei, no. 62. Decades ago, it was the practice for a sacristy to have seven colors of vestments: white, red, green, violet, black, and rose and gold or silver.
147 Sometimes called the altar platform or footpace, where the priest stands when he elevates the sacred specious.
148 II Mach. xii, 46.

Chapter Twenty

Problem   LOVE OF MONEY, POWER AND PLEASURE

Solution   LOVE FOR THE PRIESTHOOD

It was another hot summer day as I was deciding which kind of kale to pick up at the grocery store. A young man came up to me and asked, "Are you some kind of Monsignor?" I responded, "I am just a missionary priest." He explained, "My coworkers remarked that you were here. I have been thinking about becoming Catholic, and they mentioned that I missed you."

"Oh," I remarked, "I am a missionary priest and I like to help people like you who want to become Catholic. But I have to eat more nutritious food since I walk the streets. Walking around zaps my vitamins and minerals." He said, "I'm Connor, and I was just named the assistant manager for the produce here." "Well," I answered, "I am glad that you guys are non-GMO."

After explaining the produce, he told me he has been going to a Catholic Church and talking to some Catholics there, I asked, "Do you like the Latin Mass?" To which he exclaimed, "Yes, I love it!" I encouraged him, "Go to the Latin Mass this Sunday at 11:30. It is at my parish, where I was baptized. And say hello to my Mom and Dad, who will be there."

If the world would listen more to orthodox priests, the world would be a greater place in which to live. I hope that Connor listened to my words of encouragement to become a

Catholic. Priests are called to be the holiest things on earth. On the qualities of men required to receive the Sacrament of Holy Orders, St. Thomas quotes St. Jerome, "...it is most disastrous to the Church if the laity be better than the clergy."[149] The laity are not ordained priests; the clergy include all the orders[150] including the priesthood. They have to be holy so that others will be encouraged to follow them. Priests show people to God. This is the system that God placed in the world for people to come to God. He uses intermediaries.

As with all the sacraments, St. Thomas explains, "...he who being conscious of mortal sin presents himself for Orders is guilty of presumption and sins mortally."[151] He also goes on to explain how important it is for men to be holy. A priest is primarily responsible for bringing the Body and Blood of Christ onto the altar and to communicate that to Catholics in the state of grace. This is the fruit of the new tree of life. The old tree of life in Genesis gave immortality to Adam and Eve if they ate of it. But due to their sin, they were cast out of the garden and were prevented from taking of the tree of life. They became mortal – prone to death. The new tree of life is the flesh and blood that Jesus mentions in St. John chapter 6, the flesh and blood of Himself. The sacred minister who confects this fruit is a priest, and he who touches holy things must be holy, and he who leads people to heaven must be righteous.

St. Alphonsus Liguori, in his *Dignities and Duties of the Priest*, writes extensively of the exalted office of the priest. "Priests are chosen by God to manage on earth all His concerns and interests. 'Divine,' says St. Cyril of Alexander, 'are the offices confided to priests'...The entire Church cannot give to God as much honor, not obtain so many graces as a single priest by celebrating a single Mass; for the greatest honor that the Church without priests could give to God would consist in offering to Him in sacrifice the lives of all men. But what value are the lives of all men compared with the sacrifice

---

149 ST, III, Q. 36, Art. 1.
150 Porter, Lector, Exorcist, Acolyte, Sub-Deacon, Deacon, Priest, Bishop. The word 'order' can mean power.
151 ST, III, Q. 36, Art. 1.

of Jesus Christ, which is a sacrifice of infinite value?"[152] The priest has another power that is less than the power of offering the sacrifice of Jesus Christ to the Father in heaven. That is in hearing Confessions. "With regard to the mystical body of Christ, that is, all the faithful, the priest has the power of the keys, or the power of delivering sinners from hell, of making them worthy of paradise, and of changing them from slaves of Satan into the children of God."[153]

The dignity of the priest surpasses all other created dignities. "Thus the sacerdotal dignity is the most noble of all the dignities in this world. 'Nothing,' says St. Ambrose, 'is more excellent in this world.'[154] 'It transcends,' says St. Bernard, 'all the dignities of kings, or emperors and of angels.'[155] According to St. Ambrose, the dignity of the priest as far exceeds that of kings, as the value of gold surpasses that of lead.' "[156, 157]

Why is a priest considered by Catholic Saints as the greatest of created dignities? Because God in His divine wisdom chose to create other Christs[158] through the power of the Sacrament of Orders instituted by Jesus Christ. Jesus in the sacraments borrows the lips, the vocals, the hands, the entire man, consecrated as a priest when he says the words of institution at the Most Holy Sacrament of the Altar, *Hoc est enim Corpus Meum,*[159] and at other sacraments. The priest is called *sacerdos*. St. Antonine says that the meaning of *sacerdos* is *sacra docens*, one that teaches sacred things.[160] And Honorius of Autun says that *presbyter* signifies *præbens iter*, one showing the way.[161]

When a priest does his job by fulfilling the duties of his

---

152 Liguori, St. Alphonsis de, The Dignity and Duties of the Priest, Redemptorist Fathers, 1927, p. 25.
153 Ibid., p. 27.
154 De Dignit. Sac. c. 3.
155 Serm. ad Pastor. In syn.
156 De Dignit. Sac. c. 2. §§
157 The Dignity and Duties of the Priest, p. 29.
158 Alter Christus.
159 For this is My Body.
160 "Sacerdos -- Sacra docens." Summ. p. 3, tr. 14, c. 7, § 1
161 "Presbyter -- præbens iter." Gemma an. 1. l. c. 181.

office as pastor, teacher, or missionary, and tries his best to be holy, he receives the grace and light from God to teach and to lead people into heaven. He is able to direct people to God in spiritual direction. Only the fool tries to lead himself. Even priests ask other priests to be guided, to show them the way. If you ask a holy priest who fulfills his duties, you will be guided by God, because God gives the light of direction to priests. Since God has many enemies, starting with Lucifer and his dominions, it is no wonder that these enemies try every tactic to destroy the image of priests, even by having unholy and unworthy men assume the office of the priesthood. But we can never let anyone get in between us and Jesus.

What are some essentials for us to remember about the priesthood? First, pray for priests, that they be faithful and holy and that more accept the calling. Honor priests by ancient customs. Catholics used to greet a priest by taking his hand and kissing the top of it. This signifies the power of his hands to consecrate the sacred species on the altar. In some countries people show their respect for the priesthood by taking the hand of a priest and placing it on their forehead.

What happened to Connor? In a perfect world, he would have gone to the sung Latin Mass at my home parish. Then he would have taken my advice in converting to the Catholic Church. After that, he would have persevered in his resolve to be led by sacred teachings and to go the way the priest showed him. Then after his death, he would go to heaven. So what happened in actuality? My parents did not see him, but the church was packed with Mass goers. All of them received the new fruit of eternal life, the Body of Jesus Christ, a pledge of immortality, from the hands of the priest.

Chapter Twenty-One

Problem UNJUST ACCUSATIONS

Solution JUSTICE FOR THE ACCUSED AND THE SLANDERER

One day I was buying some groceries when a rude family came up to me and said, "Pedophile!" I was taken off guard, responded in silence, and realized, "Oh, I'm wearing my cassock as usual, and I should expect to receive this evisceration from time to time." What did I do next? Read the rest of the chapter.

For the last two decades, priest scandals have been front page news. Any priest that does immoral sexual things with an adult or a child is always wrong. The sins against children are the worst because the priest, who was ordained to lead people to God and be a spiritual father to the flock, abandons his post and greatly damages children who are still in their formative years. Priests are supposed to be men of prayer who spend ample time with God on a daily basis. How can priests lead people to God if they themselves do not go to God and spend time with Him in front of the Holy Altar, reciting the Psalms in the Divine Office and praying the Rosary? There is much need to confront those clergy who abuse their power. "And whosoever shall scandalize one of these little ones that believe in me; it were better for him that a millstone were hanged about his neck, and he were cast into the sea."[162] Justice is the virtue whereby each is given his due. If priests violate their sacred duty, they must receive their due punishment for the sake of their conversion to moral ways and for the common good, including the good of the Catholic Church.

At the same time, I know of priests who are faithful to their sacred duty. But because they stand up for the rights of Christ our King, they get treated with hatred. This is to be expected because the way of Christ leads to the cross, to suffering. I know many innocent priests who have been the object of unjust accusation. One pastor I know was simply telling his flock about the dangers of hell and the number of the saved. For that he was attacked on all sides. His people were not adequately catechized, so instead of taking the words of salvation to heart, they were like sheep who attacked the shepherd. One of the members even spoke openly to other members of the church that this priest was spending time inappropriately with her daughters when in fact he was doing nothing of the sort. The stories I know would fill this book and would not help bring across the point. What is unjust accusation?

First, it is important to point out that it is a matter of justice to *denounce* an evil doer and declare his fault openly in hope that he may mend his ways. To *accuse* a man is to declare his fault for the purpose of seeing him punished. Yet even punishment leads to amendment – if not always for the one subjected to it, at least for the commonwealth. Punishment in this world should be medicinal. If a man knows of a crime against the common good, already committed or being plotted, he is obliged to make due accusation, provided he can back it with proof.[163]

Second, rash accusation is sinful, for it involves calumny, collusion, or evasion. Calumny is a false charge. Collusion is fraud or trickery on the part of the accusers when there are two or more. Evasion is the making of a charge and then trying to shift out of the inconvenience that follows for the accuser. The common good is hurt by calumny, collusion, and evasion. Hence rash accusation is always unjust.[164]

Lastly, an accuser who fails to prove his charge has

---

162 St. Mark ix: 41.
163 St. Mark ix: 41.
164 ST II-II, Q. 68, A. 3.

unjustly put a man in danger of penalty. Such an accuser should be himself penalized.[165]

There is a distinction between backbiting and unjust accusation as was mentioned in Chapter 8. St. Thomas says that an accusation intends to punish someone for a crime. So the inverse follows. An unjust accusation intends to punish someone who has committed no crime. This is done openly and usually in court, whereas backbiting is done in secret, injuring the good name of a person. Reviling is done outwardly to injure a person's honor.

What if one has found himself unjustly accusing a priest? He must go to Confession with a contrite heart, ask for forgiveness from God, go to the priest to apologize, and then publicly retract the accusation or denouncement. I have rarely, if ever, seen any unjust accusers publicly retract the accusation or denouncement.

So many priests are unjustly accused of horrible crimes. What usually happens is they are no longer allowed to bring the sacraments to people, their reputation is damaged for their whole life, and the great amount of good that they may have been able to do in their lifetime is greatly hampered. The unjust accuser is responsible for preventing all the good the priest may have been able to do. Think of all the conversions the priest may have made through preaching, or all the people who may have been baptized. Think of the people who apostatized due to false accusations. There is a heaven and hell, and we are rewarded for the good we do and punished for the evil we do. The priest is the greatest of all created dignities. To falsely accuse a priest is no slight offense to God. "Touch ye not my anointed: and do no evil to my prophets."[166]

---

165 ST II-II, Q. 68, A. 4.
166 Ps. civ: 15.

Chapter Twenty-Two

Problem BELIEVING WE ARE LIKE ANIMALS

Solution UNDERSTANDING OUR HUMAN DIGNITY

I met a young man who claimed that we cannot control animalistic urges. He concluded that we cannot stop impurities and are just like dogs.

He is wrong. There is a hierarchy in creation. We see the lowest things, rocks, then plants, then animals, then humans. Each level has more powers and thus is higher in the creation. Many psychologists explain that humans cannot control some of their actions. When it comes to sinful acts like impurities, they encourage their clients to act out when the urge arises. But this way of reasoning destroys our ability to choose good and avoid evil. When we commit sinful practices, we become weaker to the passions. The passions move us to good or perceived good, like thirst moves us to a glass of water. Since we have a fallen nature due to the Original Sin of Adam and Eve, we are prone to choose lesser goods over greater goods. What this means is that we are weak, and it is easy to engage in sinful activities, speak evil words, or think evil thoughts. When we do, say, and think evil on a regular basis, it becomes a habit called a vice. Our actions form habits in us, and when we perform bad habits, we become people of vice. When we perform good habits, we become people of virtue.

St. Thomas asks, "Is choice to be found in irrational animals?" The answer is "no." St. Thomas explains the difference between the sensitive appetite and the will. The sensitive appetite moves a dog to a good. For example, when a hungry dog sees a steak, it will try to eat the steak. The sensitive appetite moves by nature. The dog does not deliberate whether to wait to eat the steak in case it is presented with ice cream a few minutes later. Nature moves the dog to try to eat the steak because survival is a part of its nature and steak helps it survive.

But there is a different power that moves human beings. It is called the will. Whereas the sensitive appetite moves the dog to the steak, the human being also has the same sensitive appetite to move it to desire the steak. But since human beings are rational, they have another step in the process. They either will or do not will the steak. Although a hungry vegetarian is moved by the sensitive appetite to eat the steak, she wills not to eat it for another good. She thinks it is better to wait for the avocado salad because she is aware of the greater nutrition. St. Thomas explains how the power of the will works: "...although determinate to one thing in general, viz., the good, according to the order of nature, is nevertheless indeterminate in respect to particular goods."[167]

In other words, the vegetarian sees both the steak and the avocado salad as food that helps survival, just as the dog sees steak and chicken for survival. What moves the dog to eat is nature alone; what moves the vegetarian to eat is nature and choice. The dog chooses the steak over the chicken because nature moves it. The vegetarian chooses the avocado salad over the steak because of her rational choice. She has been informed of the difference in nutritional value and makes an informed decision based on intellect and will. St. Thomas concludes, "Consequently choice belongs properly to the will, and not to the sensitive appetite which is all that irrational animals have. Wherefore irrational animals are not competent to choose."[168]

This whole discussion has grave importance. If a man thinks that he can commit adultery based on the false assumption that he is not free to choose, like a dog, then he is deprived. He

---
167 ST I-II, Q. 13, A. 2.
168 Ibid.

is setting himself up for a dishonorable life without nobility and is projected to be cast into eternal damnation. Therefore, we are responsible for our choices. They have eternal consequences. God will either punish evildoers to hell or reward the virtuous to heaven for eternity.

What happened to the young man who believed we cannot control animalistic urges? I listened to his argument and explained to him how we are free to make decisions, unlike dogs. They are moved by nature, and we are moved by nature and then choice. We have the freedom to choose a good out of various goods. We commit sin when we chose a forbidden pleasure, because we are free to choose something more noble, namely in this case, purity.

Chapter Twenty-Three

Problem TOO FEW PEOPLE TRULY KNOW GOD

Solution THE CHURCH GIVES PEOPLE THE CAPACITY TO ENJOY GOD

I met a sculptor in Oklahoma whose son is in a religious community. He related a recent experience his son had in the Bronx, New York.

"My son and his Community brothers, sisters, and priests went walking around the Bronx. There was this young man who read in the Bible about the Apostles going around spreading the news of Jesus Christ, the miracle worker, the Son of God and the Redeemer. So he began walking around the city speaking about Jesus Christ. Then one day he saw my son's Community and said, 'Are you the ones who are like St. Paul and Peter, whom I have been reading about in the Bible? I read about them and decided to go out and proclaim the good news of the Messiah. Are you followers of Jesus and apostles of him?'"

I will come back to the conclusion of the story of this young man. Saint Thomas Aquinas said, "Perfect Beatitude consists in enjoying God."[169] He wrote this in the *Summary Against the Gentiles* which was written to convert pagans to Christianity. The problem is that too few people truly know God. That is because too few people who *do* know God do not go out like St. Peter, St. Paul, and the son in the story at the beginning of this chapter.

---

169 SCG 4, Ch. 54

Charity is spreading the love we have received so that others may enjoy happiness. Too few Catholics tell men, face to face, that perfect happiness is enjoying God. Enjoyment is human nature, but it is not always clear what is the best way to enjoy. Some turn to food, others to sex, or others to gambling. But enjoying God is the perfect and the best way to happiness. How is it that we do well to enjoy God?

First, "Enjoying God must be desired (so we can tend to it)," St. Thomas continues. Second, "Desire arises out of love for God." Third, "Love of God must be incited." Fourth, "Love is excited by being loved." Fifth, "Man is shown that he is loved by God because He willed to be united to man in Person."[170] Why did Christ suffer the passion? It is so that man knows how much he is loved by God.

An example will help illustrate the point. Between the ages of five and fourteen, it is very important for a boy to experience the love of his father. This is required to make him whole. This is according to how God made it. If a boy asks to play catch with his dad, but dad is always "too busy," this will impair the boy's growth in maturity. He will turn out to be like his dad as we hear in some pop music songs, "My son, he became like me." Namely, the son grew up and did not have time to spend with his dad. He will learn that it is not important to spend time with his son when he grows up. But the best father spends time with his son. It is not so much as saying, "Son, I love you," which is helpful, but more importantly, it is spending quality time with the boy. Going on long walks, hunting for golf balls, and going to Church together, these are the real formative things a good father can do for his dear son. The superior is loving the inferior. The father is loving the son. The son naturally looks up to the father and gives his love. But when the father gives love to his son, it means that he is bursting with love and willing to share that.

This is how the relationship should be for all of us to God, our Father. And God the Father decided to communicate this love by way of mediation. That means that he calls leaders to mediate between Him and the people, like a priest to the people. God the Father sent his only Son to reveal His love to us. Jesus

---
170 Ibid.

only did what the Father told him to do. Jesus set up the Church to communicate His love to us first by way of the Apostles, like St. Peter and St. Paul. And there is a direct succession, called apostolic succession, where this office to preach and baptize the nations has been passed on by Peter to his successor, and then to his successor after him, all the way to the bishops and priests we know today.

Now the problem is, we have roughly seven billion people in the world and we do not have enough people transmitting that perfect beatitude consists in enjoying God. Namely the Church that Jesus gave to us, the Catholic Church, does not have enough missionaries to convert the world to Him.

Where are the saintly apostles we had in the first century? The Catholic Church has all the answers to the world's problems. Why isn't she spreading the truth that perfect beatitude consists in enjoying God?

Now how did the rest of the story above go? The young man who saw the religious propagating the faith in the Bronx stated his desire for conversion. He wanted to join the Church that the Acts of the Apostles inspired in him. Because of his faith, he is now receiving instructions on the Father's love for him. His path to heaven is now going to be simpler because, before he was going to God blindly, but now he has signposts, given to him by the visible Catholic Church instituted by Jesus Christ to save souls.

Chapter Twenty-Four

Problem LACK OF HAPPINESS

Solution THE INCREDIBLE CATHOLIC MASS

Agatha read my debut book, *Walking the Road to God: Why I Left Everything Behind and Took to the Streets to Save Souls*. She phoned me and asked, "Is it true that anyone can become a Catholic?" I said, "Of course. The word *Catholic* means universal."

Over the next four months, she received instructions and began attending the Holy Sacrifice of the Mass. She was searching for greater happiness. The rest of her story follows.

The greatest thing in the world given to us by God is the Catholic priesthood. God our Father has given his priests the power to offer the perfect holocaust of His Son our Lord Jesus Christ to Him every day. This sacrifice is acceptable to God because it is a perfect offering of His Son, the second Person of the Trinity. It is God's plan to give us His grace, His goodness, from this perfect offering. We need this in a broken world full of unhappiness.

One of my favorite books is *The Incredible Catholic Mass* by Fr. Martin von Cochem. He was a Conventual Franciscan (1630 - 1712) who promoted the canons of the Council of Trent. He lists seventy-seven graces for those who assist at the Holy Sacrifice of the Mass. I present some of those, especially the ones that will bring more happiness to the reader.

"For your salvation God the Father sends His beloved Son from heaven."[171] Our salvation means we make it to heaven. Seeing God and being with Him is a beauty and happiness beyond what we can imagine.

"For you Christ offers Himself as the most efficacious peace-offering, interceding for you as earnestly as He interceded for His enemies on the Cross."[172] It is so good for us to meditate on the Biblical scene at Calvary, where Jesus died on the Cross. When we go to the Holy Sacrifice of the Mass, God allows us to mysteriously be there and receive the fruits of adoring Jesus as he is dying on the cross. Jesus is the fruit of the new tree of life and he gives eternal life to those who eat His flesh.[173] Having a sense that Jesus who is God gives us a share of His life, we mysteriously participate in His divine life as we are in the state of His grace, having no mortal sin on our soul. That is why only Catholics who are in the state of grace are allowed to receive the Body of Jesus Christ. He changes us when we receive Communion to be more like Him, and we become more like Him each day according to our generosity. What happiness awaits those who attend Holy Communion frequently!

How many times do we call for mercy during the daily struggles in life? "Each of the adorable wounds His Sacred Body bore is a voice calling aloud for mercy for you."[174] Imagine the Son of God, who is omnipresent, can intercede to the Father on our behalf, making our struggles more bearable. The Father is pleased with the pleadings of His Son and will answer all his entreaties to alleviate our burdens if they be for our good. And our good Mother, the Blessed Virgin Mary, also intercedes for us to her Divine Son for mercy, especially at the Holy Sacrifice of the Mass. What a wonder to have such loving persons who look over us, bringing us happiness, for those who make the attendance of the Holy Sacrifice of the Mass a habit.

"If you hear Mass in the state of mortal sin, God offers

---

171 Cochem, Fr. Martin von, *The Incredible Catholic Mass*, Tan Books and Publishers, Rockford, Illinois, 1997, p. 69.
172 Ibid., p. 71.
173 St. John vi, 55.
174 Ibid., p. 71.

you the grace of conversion."[175] We sometimes slip into mortal sin, but we can come back to grace by God's mercy. We should never take mortal sin lightly because God owes us nothing when we attack His Divine Majesty. A man may be in the state of grace, steal a wallet full of cash, and then shortly get hit by a bus, dying and going to hell in mortal sin. We must always preserve the state of grace as it is the difference between eternal punishment or eternal reward.

In addition, a non-Catholic may attend the Mass without receiving Holy Communion. God gives prevenient grace, the grace of conversion for those who attend the Mass with an open heart.

"Through your diligence in hearing Mass, you will also obtain corporal and temporal blessings."[176] This is not the "health and wealth gospel" that some Protestants speak of where richness and health is a sign that one is a member of the elect. No, rather this is the Catholic view that if it be for their happiness here and salvation after this life, God rewards those who frequently adore Him at Mass with health and wealth. If it be for our good, God rewards us for giving Him the perfect sacrifice in this life and the next.

It is a dreadful thing to think of our particular judgment. When our body and soul separate at death, the time of mercy ends, and the time of judgment comes. Our good Lord Jesus will come in justice, weighing our good and our bad. "They (the Masses) will not be forgotten when you stand before the strict judge and will incline Him to show you favor."[177] When we stay in the state of grace and consistently assist at the Holy Mass, our thoughts of the Four Last Things, including our particular judgment, instead of being dreadful thoughts, will be much calmer.

"You will attain a high place in Heaven, which will be yours for eternity."[178] Imagine the city of Heaven. There are different dwelling places, some larger, some smaller, some more magnificent, some simple, others tall, and some short. The dwelling

---

175 Ibid., p. 73.
176 Ibid., p. 73.
177 Ibid., p. 74.
178 Ibid., p. 74.

places are all beautiful. Imagine our bodies and souls. Some will be more beautiful than others. Some will be closer to the likeness of God. What we do at Mass determines what happens to us now and in the afterlife. What a happy thought to give it our best every day and store up riches in heaven by attending Mass.

What happened to Agatha? She got sick and was told she was to die if she did not get surgery. She had only gone to four months of private instructions to become Catholic. The priest gave her all the sacraments on the way to the hospital since she was in danger of death. She went to the hospital and as she was going under general anesthesia for surgery, the doctor looking at her x-ray said, "Why is this woman here?" She had a miracle healing from receiving the sacraments! Our good God is still providing miracles today because he loves us dearly. As of last month, she told me that she has received Communion at the Holy Sacrifice of the Mass 202 times!

Chapter Twenty-Five

Problem CURSES, SPELLS AND SINS AGAINST THE FIRST COMMANDMENT

Solution DELIVERANCE CONTAINED IN THE HOLY PRIESTHOOD

Once someone told me that a priest at the United States Conference of Catholic Bishops stated that one fourth of the Gospels speak of Jesus driving out the demonic. I am not able to verify that exactly, but it rings true since instances of Jesus casting out of demons is quite prevalent in Holy Scripture.[179]

While I was walking around town, there was a certain man who honked as he passed by me, and I gave him the blessing. He then asked me to come to his house, for he and his wife had seen various manifestations of evil spirits throughout the home. I set up a time and decided to visit the home.

I rang the doorbell, and after we were greeted, I said the prayer, "*Pax huic domui. Et omnibus habitantibus in ea.*" Peace be to this house. And all who dwell within it.

I observed filth everywhere, and symbols of the demonic, probably more or less unbeknownst to them: a staff mounted

---

[179] Mk. i. 21-28, iii. 20-30, v. 1-17, ix. 38; Mt. viii. 28-34, xii. 22-32; Lk. iv. 31-37, viii. 27-39, ix. 49, xi. 14-23. In a word about one-seventh of the synoptic gospels.

by a skull and bones, a picture of two people flipping off the camera, a room filled with broken electronics, artificial and dark art, television screens, etc.

Each of the two residents of the house explained what they were seeing; beasts crawling on the ceiling, spirits on her back, black shadows entering the front door, all kinds of noises, doors closing without explanation, heavy objects flying off the tables, on and on. I hear these things often.

As each was relating what was happening, the grandchildren arrived from school. I began to preach the Good News, "Only two races of creatures have free will -- angels and humans...There was a war in heaven and St. Michael drove out the devils...God has them live in Hell, but he lets them roam the earth and come into our imagination to tempt us and to appear and oppress us. The ancient serpents lost their thrones in heaven and we humans, who love and serve God, will take those thrones from them some day. Satan is jealous and wants us in his kingdom, which is called Hell. He has his evil things: Ouija boards, bad rock and roll music, profanity and blaspheming. But God has His good things. Blessed candles when lit send off the blessing of the wax in the air driving away the demons of profanity. I walk these streets to encourage people to come to the gates of heaven, the Holy Altars of God. These evil things are gates to Hell.

Adam and Eve sinned by disobedience. They could have lived forever if they obeyed. They had the Tree of Life in Paradise. They were cast out of Paradise, never allowed to eat of the Tree of Life, which would have given them eternal life.[180] Thousands of years later Our Lord Jesus Christ died on a Tree, and he is the new Tree of Life. If we eat His flesh, we shall live forever.[181] The enemy of Jesus does not want you to come to the Holy Altars of God where you can become immortal. He wants you to die in sin and be tortured in eternal fire in Hell forever."

After I preached the Kingdom of God to them, I sang the "*Asperges me...*" (Sprinkle me...) and sprinkled the house with holy water. After I finished the rite of the blessing of a house, I felt

---

180 Gn. iii: 24

181 Jn. vi: 52.

peace in the house, as I do every time. I handed out Miraculous Medals and Rosaries to everyone. I invited the young man to have dinner at our refectory some day and then I left.

Chapter Twenty-Six

Problem THE WORLD HAS BECOME TOO MATERIALISTIC

Solution RETURN TO THE SUPERNATURAL

Once a student said to me, "If I cannot see it, then it does not exist." I responded by quoting Archbishop Fulton Sheen who said "it is a sign of our times that fewer men put faith in the priest who is the ambassador of God, speaking about our invisible God and the path that leads to eternal bliss with Him; and more men believe in the scientist who explains the visible world. For example, when a scientist sees under the microscope the proton of the hydrogen atom, people believe him even though they have never seen the hydrogen proton themselves. Yet when the priest speaks about the love of God, people tell him, 'show me God and then I will believe in the love of God.'" Unfortunately, people have lost the sense of the supernatural and believe in only the natural.

St. Thomas starts his work on the angels by stating that angels speak with each other. Inferior angels speak to superior angels and to God. It is written, "The angel of the Lord answered and said: O Lord of hosts, how long wilt Thou not have mercy on Jerusalem?"[1] Distance is not a hindrance to their speech and angels can speak alone to each other.[2]

There are three hierarchies of Angels and they have three subdivisions according to nature and are ranked highest to lowest in the following order: Seraphim, Cherubim, Thrones, Dominations, Virtues, Powers, Principalities, Archangels, Angels. These natures will endure forever.[3]

Angels have the ability to move things. St. Gregory says, "In this visible world nothing takes place without the agency of the invisible creature."[4] But they cannot work miracles.[5] God alone works miracles.[6]

Angles move men by enlightening them.[7] Angels cannot move the will of man, but they can change man's imagination and his senses. "To change the will belongs to God alone, according to Prov. xxi. 1: 'The heart of the king is in the hand of the Lord, whithersoever He will He shall turn it.'"[8] So angels cannot force us to do good and demons cannot force us to do evil. So how do angels influence us?

Angels reveal things to us in dreams like when the angel appeared to St. Joseph in a dream. Demons can place images in our minds, for example, images of impurity. We call these temptations of the flesh. As the old saying goes, temptations are wrought by the world, the flesh and the devil. Angels can also change human senses like when the people of Sodom experienced blindness and could not find the door.[9]

In holy Scripture the angels who are sent to guard men

---

1 Zach. i. 12
2 ST I, Q. 107, A. 1-5.
3 ST I, Q. 108, A. 1-8.
4 Dial. iv. 6.
5 A miracle is defined by St. Thomas when something is done outside of the order of nature. When angels move things according to their nature, this is not a miracle but a natural power they possess.
6 ST I, Q. 110, A. 1-4.
7 Demons cannot enlighten for they are darkness
8 ST I, Q. 111, A. 2
9 ST I, Q. 111, A. 1-4.

are called guardian angels. Each person receives a guardian angel at birth. According to Dionysuis they come from the lowest class of angels. Since demons are always assailing us, a Guardian Angel will never leave or forsake a man no matter how evil he may become.[10]

Over time man has moved from naturalism 'what is natural' to secularism and away from the natural. If we ask for the gift of faith we will be able to appreciate the generosity of God seen in the order of His angels. "God is so lavish with His gifts that He chose an angel from all eternity to be, only once, the guardian angel for a specific person, even if the person lives only one instant here on earth. And he will not be a guardian angel of another."[11]

Why is God so generous by giving us each a guardian angel? We are in a spiritual war. The angelic kingdom was given a test just as we are living through a test. Lucifer was first among the angels and wanted to be like God, not by grace, but by his own nature, and not according to God's ordering.[12] He influenced other angels in his pride and they went with him and away from God, but a greater part of the angels stayed true to God.[13] According to Suarez[14] and many theologians, the angels were given a revelation of Jesus becoming man. And according to the Mystical City of God[15] they were given a triple revelation: 1) God to be adored; 2) the Divine Incarnation; and 3) the Son of God was born of a Virgin woman. In the first revelation, the demons were reluctant to adore. In the second vision they complained

---

10 ST I, Q. 113, A. 1-8.
11 Most Rev. Athanasius Schneider in conversation with Diana Montagna, Christus Vincit : Christ's Triumph Over the Darkness of the Age, Angelico Press, Brooklyn, NY, 2019, p. 287.
12 ST I, Q. 63. A. 3
13 ST I, Q. 63. A. 9
14 Suarez, De Angelis , lib. Vii, xiii.
15 Venerable Mary of Agreda, Mystical City of God : Vol. 1, The Conception, AMI Press Washington, New Jersey, 1996, p. 89-91

because the Son was not incarnated in their nature. In the third they responded with foaming at the mouth because the Virgin Mary, a mere human lower than the nature of an angel, gave birth to the Son of God. They chose not to serve God and started their own kingdom called Hell. Today they mock God and do everything they can to take us humans into their fiery kingdom hoping to cancel the redemptive act of our Divine Saviour. Since God is all-knowing and all-loving, he assigned each a guardian angel to help us in our journey to heaven.

We should consecrate ourselves to our guardian angel. We have consecrations to the Sacred Heart of Jesus, to the Immaculate Heart of Mary and to the Most Pure Heart of St. Joseph, so why not to our guardian angel? Bishop Athanasius Schneider said, "When I was young, maybe sixteen years old, I consecrated myself to my guardian angel. Oftentimes, I have asked him to accompany me in all my prayers and I especially ask him to bring me the necessary illumination to understand the Catholic faith in the right manner. In the forty years since I first made this consecration, I have experienced this help in my mind to penetrate more deeply the truths and beauty of the Catholic faith. And in these forty years, in my prayers that my guardian angel brings me the light of God and help me remain faithful to Christ, I have had the sensation and experience that one acquires a sort of instinct of what is Catholic, of what is true. I gratefully attribute this to my guardian angel and to the consecration I made to him. I have been living my consecration to my guardian angel now for more than forty years, and I can feel his silent presence, and the light he brings during prayers. So I think we have to be more conscientious in invoking the holy angels, that they might strengthen us in faithfulness to Christ and especially in the deep sense and instinct for the holiness of God.[16]

---

16 Christus Vincit, pp. 294-295.

Now regarding that student I spoke of earlier, who said if he can't see something it doesn't exist, he was joined by other students who considered themselves atheists or agnostics and they started a very heated debate with me. In the end, I kept driving home the question, "Have you seen the proton of a hydrogen atom in a microscope?" None of them could say they had seen the proton. I concluded, then, if you put faith in a scientist, what harm could it do to at least discern the faith of a priest with an open heart? In general, people of faith are happier than people without faith. We are spiritual beings. If we have true faith we believe in God and good angels. If we do not have faith we tend to believe in magic, demons, and the occult. Halloween is a good example. When Christian society was strong almost 1,000 years ago, the culture believed in the souls of some of the dead going to Heaven. All Hallows Eve was the vigil to All Saints day. In my childhood, we celebrated "All Hallows Eve" as "Halloween" and many children dressed up as ghosts, demons, or other spiritual misfits. We went around the neighborhood and received candy from the neighbors. In general our society flipped from belief as Christians to belief in the occult. Our materialism is simply a means to deliver us to the evil of the demons.

Chapter Twenty-Seven

Problem   PORNOGRAPHY
Solution   MODESTY AND PURITY

Often I would run into a homeless man who traveled in his trademark summer outfit of shorts, a backpack and no shirt. He always made a point to tearfully beg me for prayers.

Frequently a woman would walk in on our discussion, and his passions would lead him to use disrespectful, sinful, and suggestive promiscuous language. When I would talk to him alone, I made it a custom to bring up ways to help him grow in purity. It was not a good ending as you will read below.

In my view, Pornography is an epidemic. You do not need a Doctorate to see the increase of souls falling into this addiction. Children born today are in the computer age and can easily fall into this harmful practice. It is easier than one may believe. Today's generation of young people are not like the generations from the past who were born before the 1990's. Those generations did not have computers or the internet. Before the internet, a man had to go buy a porn magazine bearing the shame of the checker. Or he had to go to a brothel or an X-rated porn shop to see adult movies with sexual content. Now children in grade school get an iPhone or SmartPhone from their friends, and without even the best of parents knowing, they start viewing pornography. When this happens at such an early age, almost all get hooked on porn. They are not told that it is wrong because parents are not aware of the invasive and inconspicuous nature of the pornography industry. This is even happening to grade school girls. The souls of our youth are being mutilated by the sin of pornography.

What is the theology behind this epidemic?

St. Thomas starts with the question whether there can be virtue or vice with outward apparel. The answer is yes. Vice occurs in two immoderate ways; first, by comparison of the customs of those among whom he lives; and second, by taking too much pleasure in wearing them. One point of excess is by wearing too costly things. "If this were no fault, the word of God would not say so expressly that the rich man who was tortured in hell had been clothed in purple and fine linen."[1] However, we will focus on the topic of his second article of the question: whether the adornment of women is devoid of mortal sin. Women have a special requirement with adorning themselves: "...a woman's apparel may incite men to lust, according to scripture, 'Behold a woman meeteth him in harlots' attire, prepared to deceive souls.'[2] Nevertheless a woman may use means to please her husband, lest through despising her, he fall into adultery."[3] St. Thomas explains further that those women who have no husband or choose not to have one, or are in a state of life inconsistent with marriage, cannot give lustful pleasure to men who see them, to incite them to sin. If women adorn themselves with

---
1 ST II-II, Q. 169, A. 1.
2 Prov. vii. 10.
3 ST II-II, Q. 169, A. 2.

the intention of provoking others to lust, they sin mortally. Then he quotes from St. Augustine, who says, in summary, non-married women who adorn themselves with gold or costly attire should think how it pleases God and married women who wear the same should think how it pleases their husband. He concludes the quote, "...it is unbecoming for women, though married, to uncover their hair, since the Apostle commands them to cover their head."[4]

St. Thomas concludes by explaining this last quote concerning the head, "Yes in this case some might be excused from sin, when they do this not through vanity but on account of some contrary custom: although such a custom is not to be commended."[5]

I have heard in sermons and also have read that modern warfare uses pornography. The aggressors try to weaken a nation by flooding the media with pornography because it psychologically weakens the men, making them effeminate. Men of vice are morally weak. A morally weak nation is easier to conquer than a morally strong nation. This is evident when men are the leading role models in the family with regards to religion. The likelihood of sons and daughters to be religious when they grow up is based almost exclusively on the faith of the father. If a father is non-religious and the mother is religious, it is likely that the offspring will leave the practise of religion. If the father is religious and the mother is non-religious the offspring will likely stay in the practise of religion. The most virtuous and manly men are religious. This is evident in the Lives of the Saints and the Martyrology. The archetype is Our Lord Jesus Christ.

So what are solutions to pornography?

First women are responsible to adorn themselves modestly. Second, men and women too need to practise

---

4 ST II-II, Q. 169, A. 2.
5 ST II-II, Q. 169, A. 2.

purity. St. Thomas explains that chastity takes its name from the fact that reason chastises concupiscence, which, like a child, needs curbing. Concupiscence is "A strong desire, especially sexual desire; lust."[6] It comes from the latin word 'cupere' 'to desire.' But with regards to pornography, it is the virtue of purity that needs to be practised as well. Chastity is a general virtue relating to venereal pleasures, which is naturally sex between a man and a woman. Lust is the contrary vice. Chastity deals with sexual union, while purity "...regards ...external signs, like impure looks, kisses and touches."[7] Ever since Adam and Eve fell they were ashamed and clothed themselves because they were naked. Purity "...takes its name from pudor, which signifies shame....even the conjugal act, which is adorned by the honesty of marriage, is not devoid of shame: and this is because the movement of the organs of generation is not subject to the command of reason, as are the movements of the other external members."[8]

I remember when I was in high school a so-called "friend" drove me to the game. While we were waiting in his car for the game to start he pulled out a porn magazine and showed me. Looking at pornography my first time, I was ashamed and told him to put it away. Those images were stuck in my mind for many years. So in order to combat pornography, we need both chastity and purity. Chastity to keep the pleasures of sex away, chastised, and purity to be ashamed to see pornography. How is this done in our day?

Young people need to be taught to pray. Prayer is a great means to virtue. Virtue is strength against vice. I believe two things are happening with our youth; first, social media keeps them from learning how to pray; and second, few are teaching them how to pray. I have observed that making the total consecration to the Blessed Virgin Mary is a must for us to grow in prayer and purity today. St. Anthony Mary Claret said, "During this deluge of sin, the new ark of

---

6 "Concupiscence" The American Heritage Dictionary
7 ST II-II, Q. 151, A. 4.
8 Ibid.

the covenant is the Immaculate Heart." We need to ask our Mother to be placed into her heart like the hull of a ship. I have also observed we need to get back to the Traditional Latin Mass. When men come to this Mass, ever so new and ever so ancient, it does something to them. It is not instant for most or one hundred percent fail proof, but it is a great weapon in the arsenal against pornography. A sung High Mass occupies the senses. The smell of incense, the sound of bells, the silence during the canon, the sight of the ministers moving to a certain ancient choreographed display is like a symphony, and the sound of the human voice and the wind of the organ, in its sacred appeal, help men trapped in pornography.

Another thing that should help is reading the sermon by St. Leonard of Port Maurice "The Little Number of Those Who Are Saved." [9] I have observed a change in men when they read this sermon. It is balanced by giving the traditional stance of the number of those who are saved like St. Chrysostom explains, but it also says that God wills to save all men and that He does not abandon the sinner. "He takes him by the hand; and while he has one foot in hell and the other outside, He still preaches to him, He implored him not to abuse His graces."

Finally, it is important how one prays. God gives sufferings to those whom He loves. Ven. Archbishop Fulton Sheen said, "Every trial can make us bitter or better." When people choose to become better from suffering it strengthens their prayer life. Pray the Rosary with the intention to be in union with God. This means to reflect on the mysteries of Jesus and Mary during the Rosary. This reminds us of what He did in order to Redeem us from Hell. Go to Church and pray in front of the Altar with the Blessed Sacrament asking for union with God.

---

[9] St. Leonard of Port Maurice, "The Little Number of Those Who are Saved."

This not only trains the imagination to stay off pornographic images, but it also allows God to change the very core of your soul. God can heal your soul from all its woundedness when you open your heart to Him in contemplation. Take a Bible and read a little and put it down and reflect upon it in silence. Go to the Sacrament of Confession with the intention of sinning no more. God wants us to try not to sin by breaking his commandments. Pray binding prayers.

The following is very helpful in my experience, "In the name of Jesus Christ and the intercession of the Blessed Virgin Mary, I command you evil spirit of lust to go and worship the Holy Trinity, Father, Son and Holy Ghost; receive an attack from your nemesis[10] or nemesis; and suffer the most excruciating pain for the next twenty minutes." Get a holy and wise spiritual director. This can be a priest who can guide you until God has helped you conquer the sin of pornography. Lastly do penance and reparation for your sins of the flesh. Our Lady of Fatima, told the children to do penance for sinners.

What happened to the shirtless man. Unfortunately the last few times that I saw him he would continue with impure talk. I told him that I cannot be around that filth and I had to shake the dust off my shoes. I do pray for him at the Holy Sacrifice of the Mass. I pray for everyone that I have met or will ever meet. I do recall he was still wearing a Miraculous Medal the last time I saw him. "O Mary conceived without sin, pray for us who have recourse to thee."

---

[10] Nemesis "A saint or angel that attacks a certain demon. That saint or angel is an unbeatable rival."

Chapter Twenty-eight

Problem LACK OF REVERENCE AND DEVOTION TO GOD LEADS YOUNG PEOPLE TO REJECT RELIGION

Solution REVERENCE LEADS TO HUMILITY, JOY AND SPIRITUAL FIRE

The majority of people I meet in the streets have left religion. When I was young I assumed all forty of my cousins who were Catholic at the time would remain Catholic. However, several of them have left the Church. Today the headlines say, "Millennials are Leaving Religion and are not Coming Back." The article notes that four out of ten have left and are not coming back even after they marry and start a family. The same article depicted a hideous sanctuary in a typical American church. I fear the people are leaving because they see only surface problems and are making excuses to leave because they want to do whatever they want to do.

There are rewards and punishments in the afterlife and the devil wants to mock God and take as many of His children to his infernal kingdom as possible. The devil uses sinful people to mock God by making religion look and seem like a farce. People forget they have an immortal soul and unknowingly feed the monster of irreverence. One of the solutions to winning back these souls in great jeopardy is reverence and devotion.

Reverence comes from the Latin *revereor* meaning 'to feel awe, to revere, respect, fear.' Devotion comes from the Latin *devovere* which means to vow. St. Thomas says, "...devout persons, in a way, devote themselves to God, so as to subject themselves wholly to Him. Hence devotion is apparently nothing else but the will to give oneself readily to things concerning the service of God."[1] For example, when I was twenty-five, I was going through a conversion and seeking God. I was sent to see some monks in Oklahoma at a monastery called Our Lady of the Annunciation of Clear Creek. I was so moved by the monks kneeling on stone floors and incense so thick you could not see the walls. All I could think about was the reverence and devotion they were showing to God. I learned by their example, and it left a lifelong impression on me. I came to understand this sign of devotion reflected an outward appearance of the charity of these monks because I went on several walks with them and noted their charity in what they said and how they spoke about God. St. Thomas notes, "...charity both causes devotion (inasmuch as love makes one ready to serve one's friend) and feeds on devotion. Even so all friendship is safeguarded and increased by the practice and consideration of friendly deeds."[2]

How does reverence and devotion lead to humility? St. Thomas says, "...while in simple souls and women, devotion abounds by repressing pride."[3] External acts of reverence can lead to internal humility. Why? Our fallen nature moves us to pride. When struggling with pride, we do well to make

---

1 ST II-II, Q. 82, A. 3.
2 ST II-II, Q. 82, A. 2.
3 ST II-II, Q. 82, A. 3.

external acts of reverence to bring about internal humility. When we kneel, fold our hands, make the sign-of-the-cross, slowly, reverently and devoutly it will eventually bring humility in our soul as long we are searching for the true God. St. Thomas explains, "...God is supremely lovable...but the human mind needs a guiding hand...by means of certain sensible objects. Chief among these is the humanity of Christ, according to the words of the Preface,[4] that through knowing God visibly, *we may be caught up to the love of things invisible.*[5] God gave us his Son to dwell among us to give us an incentive to devotion. When we meditate on the life of Jesus and His loving kindness it awakens our love. He taught the Apostles how to say Mass, "Do for a commemoration of me."[6] In my experience, the Holy Mass that follows the rules from 1962 and is celebrated more frequently by Catholics of late has great reverence and devotion. When people see it for the first time, it stays with them. They note the ritual and many are aware adoration is taking place to an invisible God even if they do not fully realize it right away.

How does reverence and devotion lead to joy? St. Thomas explains what Catholic priests say in the Collect,[7] "That we who are punished by fasting may be comforted by a holy devotion."[8] When we surrender our will to God, this can bring joy and sorrow; joy because it is fitting for us to give to God Who has given us so much, and sorrow because we do not

---

4 The "Preface" is a prayer at the Holy Sacrifice of the Mass right before the canon prayers which are prayed every day at Mass and are unchanging. These words come from the Preface for Christmastide.
5 ST II-II, Q. 82, A. 3.
6 St. Lk., xxii. 19.
7 Collect for the Thursday after the fourth Sunday of Lent. The Collect is a prayer at the beginning of the Holy Sacrifice of the Mass that "collects" the rituals preceding including the sign-of-the-cross, Psalm xlii, the confession, the introductory prayer, Kyrie, eleison , and the Gloria.
8 ST II-II, Q. 82, A. 4.

yet fully enjoy God.[9] I see this when the Nuns at Benedictines of Mary Queen of Apostles celebrate the Easter Vigil Mass. I have witnessed the Nuns leave the church so happy, hugging each other, and jumping because they have just finished the great Benedictine fast which started September 14th, lasting about six months.

How does reverence and devotion lead to spiritual fire? St. Thomas quotes Ps. xxxviii .4, "In my mediation a fire shall flame out. But spiritual fire causes devotion. Therefore meditation is the cause of devotion."[10] When we meditate on the face of Jesus when he was scourged with whips ended with lions' claws, struck with a reed and mocked as a king with a red robe, when he was hanging on the cross, we should want to serve Him and renounce our sins. What is the chief reason why so many are leaving religion? It is a lack of reverence. There is a systematic attack on God from God's enemies to destroy our ritual and empty it of all meaning. But there is good news here. One of the fastest growing categories in religion is traditional Catholics coming to traditional liturgies or converting to the Catholic Church because of them. When people come and see the incense billowing to the ceiling of gothic churches, hearing Latin chants, seeing altar boys serving with the precision like a strong military, people kneeling to receive Holy Communion, and women wearing veils, it causes those who have fallen away from religion to think twice. They may think, "Maybe these people have something that I need? Maybe there is heaven and hell, and I may go to hell if I do not investigate what they believe?"

The most important thing is that we grow in our reverence which will bring about internal humility. Humility is the gate to charity.

---

11 Ibid.
12 ST II-II, Q. 82, A. 3

Lastly, I spoke with a recent convert in his twenties. He showed me his pictures of the beautiful traditional liturgies that he has photographed. He told me that he has shared these with about five hundred people and about fifteen of them have converted to the Catholic Church in these traditional circles. May my cousins see these pictures and come back to the path that leads to God and the road to heaven.

Chapter Twenty-nine

Problem IMPROPER RECREATION

Solution VIRTUE IN GAMING AND OTHER PASTIMES

When I was 42, I was given permission by one of my bishops to start a missionary community. We had four men, then I started to get insomnia and heartburn. I developed chronic fatigue symptoms and food allergies for almost two years. Part of the problem is that we did not have enough recreation. I did not know how important it was to add games to the daily schedule in order to release the tension of the day to day life of a new religious community. I had to dissolve the Community so that I could heal. Sometimes if the devil cannot get us to sin, he tries to lure us into doing too much of the good. This was an imprudential decision, but I hope that I have learned a lot from it.

Another extreme is abandoning God for games. We saw it in the arena where Christians were martyred in Rome. Romans would spend all day watching the blood bath as wild animals would eat the Christians alive. We saw it in the gymnasium where the players were naked. This promoted promiscuity. Now we have people abandoning God in lieu of going to Church on Sundays attending games instead.

What is the answer? It is a balance and St. Thomas writes how the virtue of games is the answer.

St. Thomas places this subject under the title of temperance under the subtitle of modesty: consisting in the outward movements of the body. "Outward movements are signs of the inward disposition according to Scripture, 'The attire of the body, and the laughter of the teeth, and the gait of the man, show what he is'[1]."[2]

Then He states a story from one of the Apostles. "Thus in the *Conferences of the Fathers* (xxiv. 21) it is related of Blessed John the Evangelist, that when some people were scandalized on finding him playing together with his disciples, he is said to have told one of them who carried a bow to shoot an arrow. And when the latter had done this several times, he asked him whether he could do it indefinitely, and the man answered that if he continued doing it, the bow would break. Whence the Blessed John drew the inference that in like manner man's mind would break if its tension were never relaxed."[3] No matter how important our work is, whether it is saving souls from hell, directing air traffic, or being a dad, we all need healthy recreation. God created the world in six days and what did he do on the last day? He rested. We are made in His image and we too need to rest. When we do not let the tension go eventually we will get sick in one way or another. We need to enjoy recreation because it brings us back to creation; it is "re-creation." So what are the ways we can be virtuous in games?

St. Thomas gives three points. "The *first* and chief is that the pleasure in question should not be sought in indecent or injurious deeds or words."[4] For example, although it is fun, we should not throw fireworks at each other. Of course lewd jokes are a terrible way to blow off steam. They not

---

[1] Ecclus. xix, 27.
[2] ST II-II, Q. 168, A. 1.
[3] ST II-II, Q. 168, A. 2.
[4] Ibid.

only make light of a very beautiful passion that is directed to create life, it mocks God, the very creator of procreation. Instead of recreation, it should be called anti-creation since it is not recreation. "*Another* thing to be observed is that one lose not the balance of one's mind altogether."[5] Ambrose says, "We should beware lest, when we seek relaxation of mind, we destroy all that harmony which is the concord of good works."[6] In other words, recreation should help us to come back to work refreshed and not despising it. I think everyone experiences mental block at work. Then after putting it down, enjoying some legitimate recreation comes back and breaks through the block with a brilliant idea. "*Thirdly*, we must be careful, as in all other human actions, to conform ourselves to persons, time, and place, and to take due account of other circumstances, so that our fun befit the hour and the man as Tully says."[7] When I was walking the *Camino de Santiago*, a 500-mile pilgrimage from the Western edge of France to Northwest Spain, we began to travel with a young German woman just shy of twenty. One morning I walked by an open bar and she was drinking beer for breakfast. I as an ignorant American scolded her, "You cannot drink beer for breakfast!" She simply shrugged her shoulders, and with a beaming smile replies, "Father, I am German." Yes, Germans literally drink beer for nourishment, because it is stout and has nourishment. So what was fine for her would not be appropriate for me because of culture and upbringing, in a word, I would not be used to alcohol in the morning.

    Aristotle calls the good habit of game as wittiness or making a happy turn of mind, whereby one gives words and deeds a cheerful turn. When a man restrains from immoderate fun this is called the virtue of modesty. Can there be an excess of play?

---

5 Ibid.
6 De Offic. i. 20.
7 Ibid.

St. Thomas says that excess play, "may be sometimes mortal sin on account of the strong attachment to play, when a man prefers the pleasure he derives therefrom to the love of God, so as to be willing to disobey a commandment of God or of the Church rather than forego, such like amusements."[8] This is clearly seen when Americans spend the whole Sunday at the NFL, NBA or MLB tailgating. They disregard the moral Law of giving God his due. People will go to Hell for this sin, if they do not repent and amend their lives. What is the pleasure of a few hours when one will die in mortal sin where there will be eternal tears?

Lastly a lack of mirth is a sin. "Now it is against reason for a man to be burdensome to others, by offering no pleasure to others, and by hindering their enjoyment."[9] These people are called cads, vicious, boorish and rude. "Mirth is useful for the sake of rest and pleasures it affords; and since, in human life, pleasure and rest are not in quest for their own sake...it follows that lack of mirth is less sinful than excess thereof."[10] Aristotle says, "We should make few friends for the sake of pleasure, since but little sweetness suffices to season life, just as little salt suffices for our meat."[11] In other words, it is good to be serious because this is usually required to be profitable, industrious, and in truth. But to be too serious is a flaw and will eventually cause problems.

In conclusion, I have observed that more and more young priests are either leaving their calling or getting sick. Like myself, I think part of it is from either not enjoying enough recreation because what we do is so important, or selling out for unhealthy recreation. Society in general, the world, pushes to one extreme or the other. Look at the explosion of pornography, video games, and the explosion of

---

8 ST II-II, Q. 168, A. 3.
9 ST II-II, Q. 168, A. 4.
10 Ibid.
11 Ethic. ix. 10.

other games. Also, look at how many people are overworked some working forteen, fifteen, sixteen or more hours a day. This is a recipe for burnout. What is the answer?

We need to listen to the messages from Our Lady of Fatima and Our Lady of Revelation, Rome, Italy. She is our Mother and she warned us to obey the Commandments, and to pray the Rosary for sinners. But we have not heeded her warnings and the errors of Russia have spread over the world. St. John Paul said that it is too late to avert the coming chastisement, but if we pray we can mitigate it. When we pray for the wisdom to know what games, what circumstances, what friends to make, a person in sanctifying grace will receive inspirations to have the best recreation.

Chapter Thirty

Problem   THE EVIL OF THE WORLD SEEMS TOO GREAT TO OVERCOME.

Solution   THE BLESSED VIRGIN MARY AND THE ROSARYBE

While I was suffering from a chronic illness, my doctor advised me to take two and a half hour hikes a few times a month. It is called LSD, long slow distance. I found Smithville Lake which has long winding walking paths. As I was enjoying the cool breeze and the setting sun. I glanced at my watch, noticing my half-point was arriving, so I turned around to head back. Approaching me was a middle-aged woman and her doberman pinscher, a huge dog! I thought, "This is going to be interesting." She was on her phone, but I greeted her with a "Hello." She sharply responded, "I think I saw you already." I explained, "I am just turning around."

I continued walking and noticed a park ranger truck circling in the distance about a half mile from me. It accelerated out of sight. Then moments later there was a park ranger truck behind me, on the walking path, and three other park ranger trucks descended upon me. The ranger in the rear was a corporal who got out of his vehicle and asked if I had identification. As I reached into my cape and cassock, I noticed he put his hand on the top of the gun mounted on his belt. I knew if I made the wrong move there would be trouble. After finally securing the I.D. from my wallet, I gave it to the ranger as the other three rangers approached me.

The sergeant queried, "Are you some kind of a rabbi or father?" To which I responded, "I am a Catholic Priest and a Chaplain at the Abbey of Ephesus. Ephesus is a city where St. Paul lived for a while and Mary." The female ranger curiously asked, "Who is Mary?" "Oh she is the Mother of our Redeemer," I remarked.

The corporal asked, "Do you have a weapon?" I said, "No." He asked, "Can I search you?" I said, "Yes." He could not find anything till he came to my right pocket. "What is this?" he asked. I said, "Oh I forgot to tell you I do have a weapon. It is my Rosary."

It is true that there are a lot of evil people in the world, but God's weapon to fight evil is the Blessed Virgin Mary and the weapon she has given to us is the Rosary.

I told the ranger, "I have something for you." So I pulled out of my shoulder cape, from a pocket my mother designed for purposes like this, some Miraculous Medals. I showed them the medal and said, "One man received one of these from me and told me three years later that it cured him of his alcohol addiction the day I gave it to him and he put it on."

After we were all at peace I asked them, "May I give you my blessing?" They agreed and I blessed them and departed.

When Catholic Europe was beginning to throw off the yoke of Jesus Christ during the Protestant Revolt in 1517, the Blessed Virgin Mary was soon to follow with her work of God in 1531 when, on December 9th, she appeared to St. Juan Diego on the hill of Tepeyac in Mexico. She had Juan pick some roses even though "the hill was a desert place were only cactus, thistles and thornbrush grew."[182] He brought them to Bishop Zumarraga who fell to his knees when he saw the flowers and the image of the Blessed Virgin Mary on his tilma. This was the beginning of the conversion of over nine million Aztecs to the Catholic faith. As Catholic Europe was crumbling, Mexico was converting to Christ the King and his mother was the "weapon" that God used. The Aztecs were literally turning away from the demon gods who had them killing and sacrificing so many people that blood was flowing down the Aztec pyramids like a river.

---

182 Carroll, Warren H., The Cleaving of Christendom, Vol. 4, Christendom Press, 2000, Front Royal, VA, p. 618.

Yes, the world is evil, but when we consecrate ourselves to the Immaculate Heart of Mary, we can overcome the evil with the joy of the Gospel. The Book of Wisdom chosen for the Holy Day of the Immaculate Conception explains this beautiful joy. We need to read it from the point of view of the Blessed Virgin Mary.

"The Lord possessed me in the beginning of his ways, before He made anything, from the beginning. I was set up from eternity, and of old, before the earth was made. The depths were not as yet, and I was already conceived...I was with Him, forming all things, and was delighted every day, playing before Him at all times, playing in the world: and my delight is to be with the children of men."[183]

So while the revolution against God was churning in Europe, the Blessed Virgin Mary was "playing in the world." She was drawing down the mercy of God upon the Mexican people to break them from the yoke of the stone serpent by the aroma of her virtues, calling herself, "she who crushed the head of the stone serpent."[184]

How can we "play" in the world as children before our heavenly Father? Jesus held up a child and said, "unless you be converted, and become as little children, you shall not enter into the kingdom of heaven."[185] How do we become like little children? A good father loves to see his little children playing. It is a delight to him. Our Father in heaven loves to see us playing

---

183 Prov. viii. 22-24, 30-31
184 Bishop Buddy of San Diego along with Fr. Francis Johnston The Wonder of Guadalupe and Helen Behrens explain how the Aztec language was used by the Blessed Virgin Mary to tell Juan Bernando the sick uncle of St. Juan Diego her name. The alphabet does not have a "G" or "D." When Juan Bernando who received a vision from Mary telling him her name, he related it to the Bishop and his court, but they thought he said "Guadalupe" a Marian Shrine in Spain. Many other sources explain how the Blessed Virgin Mary wished to be known as 'she who crushes the head of the stone serpent,' a reference to Gen. iii. 15.
185 St. Mt. xviii. 3

in the world. What exactly does this mean? It means imitating the Blessed Virgin Mary. When evil seemed to be triumphing, she helped convert nine million pagans. She was destroying the stone serpent. We can become like children if we take the Rosary and sincerely pray it destroys the serpents in our lives.

The Blessed Virgin Mary told St. Dominic, "I want you to know that, in this kind of warfare, the battering ram has always been the Angelic Psalter (The Hail Mary)."[186] "Blessed Alan, according to Carthagena, mentioned several other times when Our Lord and Our Lady appeared to Saint Dominic to urge and inspire him to preach the Rosary more and more in order to wipe out sin and to convert sinners and heretics…But many priests want to preach thunderously against the worst kinds of sin at the very outset, failing to realize that before a sick person is given bitter medicine he needs to be prepared by being put in the right frame of mind to really benefit by it."[187]

Saint Dominic received another revelation that reveals why priests need to say a Hail Mary out loud before preaching a sermon, "My son do not be surprised that your sermons fail to bear the results you had hoped for. You are trying to cultivate a piece of ground which has not had any rain. Now when almighty God planned to renew the face of the earth, He started by sending down rain from heaven -- and this was the Angelic Salutation." (The Hail Mary).[188]

There are bad people in the world and the woman with the big dog was scared because she probably never saw a priest in his cassock. What began as a good walk could have turned out in a bad way. But the Blessed Virgin Mary allowed me to encourage the four park rangers to go to the Catholic Church. She allowed me to give each of them a Miraculous Medal, and to impart my sacerdotal blessing. The Rosary is truly a weapon to bring good out of evil.

---

186 St. Louis de Montfort, The Secret of the Rosary, Montfort Publications, Bay Shore, NY, 1990, p. 18.
187 Ibid., p. 21.
188 Ibid., p. 21.

Chapter Twenty-one

Problem BELIEF THAT THE CATHOLIC CHURCH IS EVIL, AND THEREFORE EITHER THERE IS NO GOD OR THE TRUTH LIES IN A DIFFERENT CHURCH

Solution THE BLESSED VIRGIN MARY AND THE ROSARY

People often come to me with objections: "Father I left the Catholic Church because of Father X. Or I do not like what the Pope is saying so I gave up on the Catholic Church. Or the sexual abuse scandals are so evil that I cannot stay in a Church with such evil perverts."

Often, people need an excuse to live the way they want to live without regard to keeping God's holy Commandments. But it is important to not abandon reason and go deeper into grasping the nature of the Church, a saving institution given to us by God.

St. Hilary -- the Athanasius of the West[189] -- attacks this weak reasoning with these beautiful words. "In this consists the particular nature of the Church, that She triumphs when She is defeated, that She is better understood when She is attacked, that She rises up, when Her faithful members

---

189 Most Rev. Schneider, Athanasius, *Christus Vincit: Christ's Triumph Over the Darkness of the Age*, in conversation with Diane Montagna, Angelico Press, Brooklyn, NY, 2019, p. 305.

desert her."[190] We have to remember that God reveals His nature through our Most Holy Redeemer, Jesus Christ. He is all powerful and appears on earth as a mere baby. He is tempted by Satan in order to show us by example how to live through the devil's vile deceits. And He dies on a cross to show that triumph comes from apparent defeat. So why is it important to stay in or join the Church?

God is One, Truth, Beauty and Goodness. These are the four transcendentals, attributes of God. It follows, since He is One, that He gives us one means to approach Him and come to heaven. He gives us His only Son, True God and our Holy Redeemer to establish One, True, Catholic and Apostolic Church. He gave us one Mother, the Blessed Virgin Mother. He gave us one Vicar of Christ, one Pope, St. Peter and his successors (that is why extra "popes" are called antipopes). So it is by the very nature of God and His Oneness that he makes the nature of His Church to be one. So how does one stay in the Church? Patience.

St. Thomas gives a beautiful explanation of the virtue of patience. Quoting Scripture he writes, "The sorrow of the world worketh death,"[191] and, "Sadness hath killed many, and there is no profit in it."[192] "Hence the necessity for a virtue to safeguard the good of reason against sorrow, lest reason give way to sorrow: and this patience does."[193] Patience helps a man to bear trial with an equal mind, without being disturbed by sorrow, lest he abandon with an unequal mind the goods whereby he may advance to better things.[194] We are rational creatures, meaning that we are moved by our mind, not like brute animals that are only moved by their instincts. This ultimately means that we have a free will. We have the ability to choose good or evil. Patience is the virtue

---

190 De Trin. 7, 4.
191 II Cor. vii. 10.
192 Ecclus. Xxx. 25.
193 ST, Pt. II-II, Q. 136, A. 3.
194 St. Augustine, De Patientia ii.

that helps us to endure hardship and make good decisions. In terms of the Catholic Church, given to us for our salvation, we must remain with Her to the end of our life. She is there to help us to heaven. Patience allows us to see past the evil that is present in Her. The Church is full of sinners. But She is a means to give us grace from God to help us with every difficulty. Do we get the virtue of patience on our own or does it come from the grace of God?

"From Him is my patience."[195] Now no man in his right mind desires suffering for its own sake. Rather he is willing to suffer and bear what is painful for that which gives pleasure. For example, a man plants a garden, and endures the toil of working the soil in order that he may reap a harvest and thus eat. St. Thomas explains, "Now the fact that a man prefers the good of grace to all natural goods, the loss of which may cause sorrow, is to be referred to charity, which loves God above all things." In other words, patience is caused by charity. "Charity is patient."[196] It is impossible to have charity except through grace. "The charity of God is poured forth in our hearts by the Holy Ghost Who is given to us."[197] "Therefore it is clearly impossible to have patience without the help of grace."[198]

This is why we must remain in or join the true Church. God has chosen to help us by mediation. The Father sent the Son to redeem us. He established the Church with seven signs, the sacraments, that give us grace. Baptism establishes us as adopted sons, and as sons, we receive His help through baptism. It is through the Blessed Virgin Mary that we received Jesus our Savior. She is known as the Mediatrix of all graces. The Father decided that the only way for us to receive His Son is through our Mother the Blessed

---
195 Ps. lxi. 6.
196 I Cor. xiii. 4.
197 Rom. v. 5.
198 ST, Pt. II-II, Q. 136, A. 3.

Virgin Mary. It only makes sense if God delivered Jesus to us through her, that we should go through her to Jesus. The Church was conceived in her womb. After Pentecost, the birthday of the Church, mediation continues. It is the Bishop of Rome who is the Vicar of Christ on earth. It is through the Pope, through Mary, through Jesus, that we go to the Father. And this mediation continues through the bishop and through his priests. Even the Old Testament worship was set up with mediation. The priest was the mediator between God and the people. Moses was the mediator between God and the people when he received the Ten Commandments. The priest stands at the Altar of God, the very threshold of grace, which comes through the priest to the people. It is only through the Church that we are saved.[199]

    It is important for us to ask for patience. Patience is a gift. God gives it to those who ask. If you have left the Church, ask for patience. If you are struggling with the church, ask for patience. This present trial the Church is enduring is similar to the passion of Jesus Christ. He was patient until he died on the cross. He was denied by St. Peter. Judas betrayed Him. All the other Apostles fled except for St. John and only the Blessed Virgin Mary and the Holy Women remained at the foot of the Cross. It was worth it for them to suffer and witness Jesus die. It is worth it for us to witness the Church in Her passion and remain with Her. It is the means that God has chosen for us to enjoy eternal happiness.

---

[199] Denzinger 430, Lateran Council IV, 1215.

Chapter Thirty-two

Problem THE FALSE BELIEF THAT OUR GENERATION IS MORE VIRTUOUS THAN PAST GENERATIONS

Solution UNDERSTANDING THAT RECENT GENERATIONS HAVE GREATLY OFFENDED GOD AND HAVE RECEIVED WORSE PUNISHMENTS THAN THOSE IN THE OLD TESTAMENT

On a city bus one day, a Christian man initiated a conversation with me. "Father, I like the Old Testament better because punishment fit the crime and it was done swiftly." I did not know what to say at the time, but I have pondered his statement. On the streets in conversation with those I meet I get the general sense that the current generation thinks we are more virtuous than those of the Old Testament. This way of thinking is very dangerous because it gives one the false sense of favor with God.

In my observation, ever since the Protestant Revolt, each generation has gotten worse. God has told the people of these times through His Vicars, the Popes, how to act. But our generations have not heeded this advice, so God is punishing us with the worst punishment we have ever seen. He is giving us what we want, and we are being delivered up to our enemies. In the twenty-sixth chapter of Leviticus, God gives promises to those who keep His commandments and threatens punishment to transgressors. "I am the Lord your God: you shall not make yourselves any idol...[1]"

We are now worshiping many idols -- from material things to Pachamamas[2] -- and have fallen into multiple and varying errors. That is why St. Pope Pius X called Modernism, "The synthesis of all errors." The book of Leviticus continues, "Keep my sabbath, and reverence my sanctuary..."[3] We have lost reverence in God's house over the generations, from talking and clapping in Church, to taking Holy Communion in dirty hands.

The Word of God continues: "If you keep my commandments...the ground shall bring forth increase."[4] It may seem that we have plenty of food in the United States of America. We give the extra to the poor. But if we look closer, we may recognize the signs of a certain kind of famine. Our ground does not have the minerals it used to have. The greatest mineral deficiency in most people, according to some experts, is magnesium. The ground is tilled and over-used and magnesium is not put back into the soil. I had chronic fatigue for over a year and one of the missing minerals was magnesium. "Magnesium is an essential cofactor required by 700-800 enzyme systems that promote thousands of biochemical reactions in the body."[5] We are witnessing a different kind of famine. Toxic chemicals are sprayed on our crops and we ingest them. They enter the bloodstream of people who have a compromised intestinal system. This triggers an immune system response which causes all kinds of health problems, from inflammation to anxiety. The remedy is

---
1 Lev., xxvi, 1.
2 "Pachama" is a goddess revered by the indigenous people of the Andes.
3 Lev., xxvi, 2.
4 Lev., xxvi, 3-4.
5 Dr. Dean's ReMag magnesium drink.

eating food that is organic, which has no pesticides, chemicals or toxins. But this is very expensive. Many families cannot afford to buy organic. This is a very new type of famine. We have enough food, but people are getting sick from it.

"You shall eat your bread to the full…"[6] How many people are gluten intolerant? Gluten is a protein found in wheat that can be hard for some people to digest in the modern era because wheat has changed. "Most experts believe that foods are higher in chemicals and are different in many ways from how they were in the past."[7]

I went through some major stress in my priesthood and my doctor diagnosed me with a leaky gut and an acute chronic illness, picking up a few food allergies and intolerances that I never had before. Gluten was the biggest danger because it increases the size of the leaks and destroys the gut flora in some people whose gut is compromised. The doctor told me that, in a few more years, I would have celiac disease.

So with new mineral deficiencies, leaky gut and many new diseases, how is this different from the Old Testament? They had disease too. The biggest difference is that our punishment is not as clear as punishment in the past. King Ozias of Judah was unfaithful to the Lord and entered the temple of the Lord to burn incense. The priests forbade him since only priests were consecrated to burn incense at the altar. Ozias rose in anger and offered incense. He was struck on the forehead with leprosy at an instant when going into the sanctuary.[8] Oza was struck dead because he touched the ark when it began to fall. His hands were not consecrated and God struck him dead because only the priests and Levites were allowed to touch the ark.[9] In general, the punishment

---

6 Lev., xxvi, 5.
7 Dr. Alan Christenson, NMD, The Adrenal Reset Diet, Harmony Books, New York, 2014, p. 19.
8 II Paralipomenon, xxvi, 19.
9 II Kings vi, 7.

in the Old Testament was instant. Today the punishment is hidden and delayed. Why is this?

According to St. Thomas the "Old Law is like a pedagogue of children, as the Apostle says (Gal. Iii.24), whereas the New Law is the law of perfection, since it is the law of charity, of which the Apostle says (Coloss. Iii. 14) that it is the bond of perfection."[10] This means that we have a greater knowledge of right and wrong. Just as a baby is not held to the rules of the house as a teenager is, because the baby is young and does not know better; whereas the teenager is more responsible. So we know more than the people of the Old Testament. The punishment must fit the crime. When we transgress the New Law we are punished more severely. We have received the fullness of revelation from the Word, the veil has been removed from our eyes more than those of the Old Testament by Our Lord Jesus. The New Testament law is perfect.[11] St. John Chrysostom expounds on Mark iv. 28, "The earth of itself bringeth forth fruit, first the blade, then the ear, afterwards the full corn in the ear." The saint explains, "He brought forth first the blade, i.e., the Law of Nature; then the ear, i.e., the Law of Moses; lastly, the full corn, i.e., the Law of the Gospel." Lastly the New Law is a lighter burden than the Old Law for a man who has virtue. A virtuous man follows God with pleasure and promptitude; whereas a vicious man follows God with burden. The reason for this is charity. The virtuous man loves to follow God. Charity is poured out in the sacraments.[12] "My yoke is sweet and my burden is light."[13] So how is our punishment worse for similar offenses under the Old Law?

---

10 ST I-II, Q. 107, A. 1.
11 ST I-II, Q. 107, A. 3.
12 ST I-II, Q. 107, A. 4.
13 St. Matt., xi, 30.

When a rational thinking creature has more information to make a decision, a disobedient act is punished more severely. The angelic kingdom went through a test. They are judged by a stricter law because according to their nature they had all the information to make a decision. That is why when an angel makes a decision it will never change its mind. Demons transgressed God's law once and will never change their minds against Him. Humans transgress the law of God and often God has mercy on us. But eventually the time of grace will come to an end and we will be judged at our particular judgment. We have more knowledge of the law of God than the Old Law because Jesus revealed it through Himself. We as a human family are entering the worst age in the history of the Church since the time of Christ. According to Bishop Athanasius Schneider we are in the worst age the Church has ever witnessed, "But I believe that there could not be a worse situation in the life of the Church than the one we are now witnessing."[14] How will this end?

We have to intensely desire the charity of God to grow in us. It was bad when the St. Peter, the first Pope denied Christ and only one Apostle, St. John, was willing to suffer at the foot of the Cross. In the end there was one traitor, Judas. He had the fullness of revelation given to him in the presence of the Word. His rebellion was severely punished because he was the recipient of the New Law. According to the *Mystical City of God* there was a special place reserved for him in Hell. "Among the obscure caverns of the infernal prisons was a very large one, arranged for more horrible chastisements than the others, and which was still unoccupied; for the demons had been unable to cast any soul into it, although their cruelty had induced them to attempt it many times from the time of Cain unto that day. All hell had remained astonished at the failure of these attempts, being entirely ignorant of the mystery, until

---

14 Most Rev. Schneider, Athanasius, Christus Vincet, p. 304.

the arrival of the soul of Judas, which they readily succeeded in hurling and burying in this prison never before occupied by any of the damned. The secret of it was, that this cavern of greater torments and fiercer fires of hell, from the creation of the world, had been destined for those, who, after having received Baptism, would damn themselves by the neglect of the Sacraments, the doctrines, the Passion and Death of the Savior and the intercession of his most holy Mother. As Judas had been the first one who had so signally participated in these blessings, and as he had so fearfully misused them, he was also the first to suffer the torments of this place, prepared for him and his imitators and followers."[15]

So if I ever meet the man again on the bus, I will have something to say. After explaining the above, I hope to tell him, "I have a gift for you, the Miraculous Medal. I want to give it to you with the hope that you will embrace the saving victory of Jesus Christ who has given us the New Covenant, His Body and Blood." A sure way of eternal salvation in this crooked generation is to enter the Church of the Savior and receive his Communion the sacred body and blood and pledge for eternal life.

---

15 Ven. Mary of Agreda, Mystical City of God, Vol. 3, pp. 518-519.

Also by Father Lawrence Carney

WALKING THE ROAD TO GOD
Why I Left Everything Behind and Took to the Streets to Save Souls

Father Lawrence Carney travels the country, walking the city streets in his cassock, carrying a crucifix, praying the Rosary and seeking lost souls. In his debut work, he writes of the many people he meets, the conversations that unfold and the divine appointments arranged for a priest who lives his life entirely for the salvation of souls. He also reveals his dream of a new order of priests, clerics and brothers, who walk and pray in cities around the United States in an effort to regain what has been lost. With so many lukewarm and fallen-away Catholics in our world today, it is easy to become discouraged. But, rooted in the joy of gospel promises, Father Carney proclaims hope.

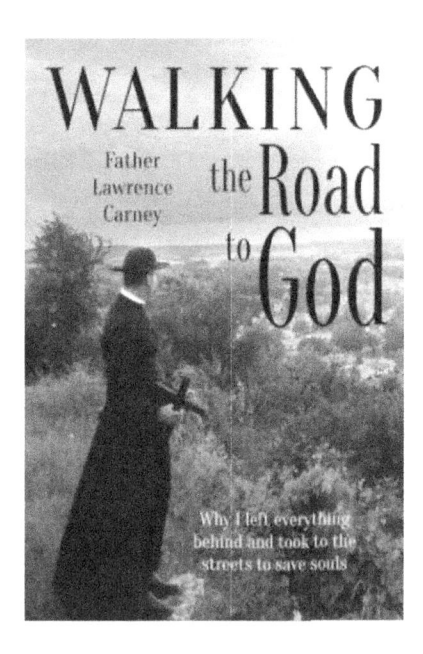

PRAISE FOR *WALKING THE ROAD TO GOD*

"There is nothing fancy or sophisticated here, but rather luminous faith and humility. Fr. Carney shares his ideas, experiences, and plans. The humility and radical charity are contagious: after reading the book in (almost) one sitting, I felt imbued with a desire to bear witness for Christ." -- Julian Kwasniewski, OnePeterFive book review

"A Masterpiece on Contemporary Street Evangelization." -- Catholic revert and evangelist Scott Woltze

"You will be fairly amazed at the beautiful seeds planted and souls converted, and the amazing circumstances encountered in this process. Even in the fallen times we live in, "Walking the Road to God" is proof-positive that one man devoted to the hearts of Jesus and Mary can turn this ship around." -- Stephen Connelly, Amazon reader review

"Father takes the Gospel right to where we live; he comes to us on the streets where Jesus encountered His flocks. Like Our Lord, Father tells stories (parables) about those he's encountered in the streets, and in doing so, he shares the faith with those he meets and those who read his book. This walking priest gives people his free time which is such a gift in our busy world to find someone who will chat with us, and he prays with us and for us." -- Judi Paparozzi, Amazon reader review

"Our post-Christian society starves for love. Many people do not know God or the things of God. The Holy Spirit shows us, through Father Carney, how to share the life of God within us with whomever we meet. This is how a Catholic should encounter another human being, giving great love, joy, respect, and hope." -- Charles Bruce, Amazon reader review

Other books from Caritas Press

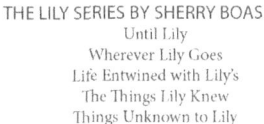

THE LILY SERIES BY SHERRY BOAS
Until Lily
Wherever Lily Goes
Life Entwined with Lily's
The Things Lily Knew
Things Unknown to Lily
A Little Like Lily

"...You will be entranced, you will experience the joys and sorrows of the characters, you will cry, and you will not be able to put Lily down."
– Dr. Jeff Mirus of CatholicCulture.org

The transforming power of love is at the heart of Sherry Boas' poignant series about the people whose lives are moved by a woman with Down syndrome. Lily's story is told with such brutal yet touching honesty, it will have you laughing one minute and reduced to tears the next.

WING TIP
A Novel

Dante De Luz's steel was forged in his youth, in the crucible of harsh losses and triumphant love. But that steel gets tested like never before as his mother's deathbed confession reveals something startling about his father and presents the young Catholic priest with the toughest challenge of his life, with stakes that couldn't get any higher.

"Aside from death and taxes, here's one more thing that is certain in this life: Sherry Boas' Wing Tip, will be a classic of Catholic literature. Magnificent read, highly recommended."

Robert Curtis,
The Catholic Sun

Laughter of Angels
By Sherry Boas

New York City journalist Verdi Leoni discovers that death looms near for the scavenger who rescued her from a garbage dump when she was a baby. So Verdi quits her job at the newspaper and returns to her native China to take care of the ailing woman. But there is someone else in Shanghai who needs Verdi even more—someone who is not so easy to love. It takes all the strength Verdi can muster to care for the caustic old man, who holds the power—but no desire—to bind the wound she harbors in the depths of her soul. With the unfolding of a number of staggering revelations, Verdi begins to understand that nothing she thought she knew can be taken for granted, not even the story of her own life.

Rosary meditations for everyone in the family

Dads   Moms   Children   Teens   Grandparents   Altar Servers   Special full-color Gift Edition and Journal for Mom

CHILDREN'S BOOKS FROM CARITAS PRESS

Caritas Best Seller ➡

SAINT JOHN BOSCO AND HIS BIG GRAY DOG
During times of danger, a very special guardian would appear to protect St. John Bosco. In this way, God saved the holy priest from harm so he could complete his mission and help children come to know God.

EMMYLOU FINDS HER VOICE
A heartfelt tale of a hen with an unusual gift -- a talent for singing that brings scornful criticism from her envious peers. Emmylou rises above the bullying and even helps another hen to embrace her own beautiful differences.

IGNATIUS OF LOYOLA AND HIS WISE HORSE
Ignatius is a valiant soldier, eager to defend the honor of the Lady who has captured his devotion. But when Ignatius's anger gets the best of him, his faithful horse must make a life-or-death choice.

By Brenda Castro & Maria Boas

Caritas Best Seller ➡

GOD'S EASTER GIFTS
A very special Easter egg hunt shows brother and sister, Pablo and Bella, that there's much more to Easter than candy and toys.

JACKIE'S SPECIAL HALLOWEEN
Sister and brother duo Bella and Pablo return in this delightful story about the true meaning of Halloween. Author Brenda Castro captures young imaginations and shows them the truth and beauty of the Faith

ENCYCLOPEDIA OF PEG SAINTS
Get to know 36 saints in an engaging and easy to "absorb" format, centered around colorful hand-painted peg dolls collected and cherished by Catholic kids everywhere.

ORDER AT CARITASPRESS.ORG OR AMAZON

By Sherry Boas

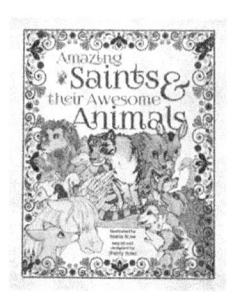

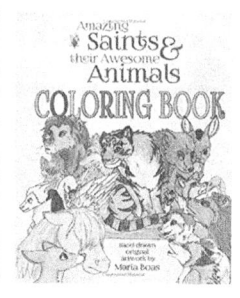

THE GIFT IN THE MANGER

When their feeding trough ends up serving as a bed for a tiny baby, the animals get a glimpse into God's loving plan to save the world. Like every one of us, each of the animals gathered around the manger has a struggle to overcome. They, like us, find the answer in Jesus, the only one who can fix our brokenness, heal our imperfections and give us the gift that makes us whole – the gift of Himself.

AMAZING SAINTS & THEIR AWESOME ANIMALS

Saints throughout the ages have loved their animal friends, and in return, the beasts have loved them back. This sampling of stories reveals the compassion, respect, and affection holy people have shown for all of God's creatures. Companion coloring book available.

BILLOWTAIL

Little creatures on a big adventure in on the Way of Saint James in medieval Spain. 220-page Novel.

ARABEL'S LAMB

A young girl's compassion is tested to the limits in this gripping tale about love and sacrifice. Loosely based on the legend of St. George and the Dragon.

ARCHANGELA'S HORSE

Archangela comes to understand God's will when her beloved and loyal horse refuses to take her where she wants to go.

By Ruth Pendergast Sissel & Tina Tolliver Matney

BARNYARD BLISS

All of creation rejoices as word of the baby owlet spreads throughout the farm from one animal to the next.

MIRACULOUS ME

A mother and father dream of the future as they celebrate the precious gift of life, the baby who is about to arrive. What will the days of her life hold?

ORDER AT CARITASPRESS.ORG OR AMAZON

Caritas Press was founded in 2011 with the mission of shedding light on things eternal in a culture that is becoming increasingly blind to the wonders of God's works and numb to His boundless love. Making use of the subtle and the beautiful, Caritas Press hopes to play a part in igniting in adults and children a desire to know God more fully. For a full listing of all Caritas titles for children, youths and adults, visit CaritasPress.org.

CARITAS PRESS
CaritasPress.org

Made in the USA
Las Vegas, NV
20 April 2025